THE LENT FACTOR

THE LENT FACTOR

FORTY COMPANIONS FOR THE FORTY DAYS OF LENT

GRAHAM JAMES

BLOOMSBURY

LONDON • NEW DELHI • NEW YORK • SYDNEY

First published in Great Britain 2014

Copyright © Graham James, 2014

The moral right of the author has been asserted

No part of this book may be used or reproduced in any manner
whatsoever without written permission from the Publisher except in the
case of brief quotations embodied in critical articles or reviews. Every
reasonable effort has been made to trace copyright holders of material
reproduced in this book, but if any have been inadvertently overlooked
the Publisher would be glad to hear from them.

A Continuum book

Bloomsbury Publishing Plc
50 Bedford Square
London WC1B 3DP

www.bloomsbury.com

Bloomsbury is a trademark of Bloomsbury Publishing Plc

Bloomsbury Publishing, London, New Delhi, New York and Sydney

A CIP record for this book is available from the British Library.

ISBN 9781408184042

10 9 8 7 6 5 4 3 2

Typeset by Fakenham Prepress Solutions, Fakenham, Norfolk
NR21 8NN

Printed and bound in Great Britain by CPI Group (UK) Ltd, Croydon
CR0 4YY

For Julie,
life's companion

Permissions

Excerpts from the following are reproduced by kind permission of the publishers.

Charles Causley, 'Timothy Winters' and 'Ballad of the Bread Man' from *Collected Poems* (London: Macmillan, 1975)

U. A. Fanthorpe, 'Lostwithiel in February', 'Angels Song' and 'The Wicked Fairy at the Manger' from *New and Collected Poems* (London: Enitharmon Press, 2010)

Judith Wright, 'Grace' from *A Human Pattern: Selected Poems* (Sydney: ETT Imprint, 2010)

Contents

Contents

INTRODUCTION

The media trades in human interest stories because most of us are fascinated by other people, even those we have not met. Celebrity gossip has become an industry in itself, spawning magazines and websites devoted to nothing else. The old-fashioned talent show has been transformed into a glamorous contest, as in *Britain's Got Talent* and a host of other series. New stars have been born though sometimes they make only a fleeting appearance in the celebrity sky. *The X Factor* proved the biggest of all such contests. X represents star quality and hidden gifts, a mysterious attribute which is a seam of pure gold. It only needs exposure and everyone sees how it gleams. The use of X in this context is no accident. X has been traditionally used as a mark of identity. It is deeply personal. Those unable to read or write, marked documents, including marriage registers, with an X. X became the mark we use on ballot papers, itself a consequence of a hitherto largely illiterate nation. For Christians, X has another dimension. It is the symbol of salvation. The character of God is revealed supremely by Jesus Christ suffering and dying for humanity on the cross. Down the centuries Christians have gazed at the Cross, prayed before it, pondered the passion narrative, and found their own identity redeemed and enlarged. X is a potent and many-layered symbol.

This book describes 40 people whose human identity I have found compelling. They are not flawless. I recall one definition of a saint as 'someone in Christian history whose life has been insufficiently researched'. That's a reminder that saints are also sinners like the rest of us. Those who inspire faith in others, or lead us to want to imitate their best qualities, are not without blemish. Some of the people included in this book led astonishingly active lives and achieved great fame. Others are much less well known. Some are hardly known to anyone except in my family. With some I have had a deep personal connection. Others were dead long before I was born.

If human beings are made in the image and likeness of God (Genesis 1.26) then we should expect to see God's nature reflected in our fellow men and women. These daily companions, particularly chosen for Lent, but with whom the reader can travel at any time, fall into no particular category, though what they have in common is influence in my own life. I am Cornish by origin from a family whose roots lie in the tin-mining district between Camborne and

Redruth. My parents grew up in a working-class tin-mining culture and on my father's side there was very little church-going tradition at all. By the time of my birth he had left the mining industry and had become a Congregationalist minister. When I was 11 I witnessed his ordination in the Church of England at Peterborough Cathedral and was ordained there myself 13 years later. An early ministry in two council estate parishes was followed by work at Church House, Westminster and Lambeth Palace before my consecration as a bishop in 1993. I met my wife, Julie, when she was completing her training as a midwife in Peterborough and she continues to work in nursing, now in palliative care. We have had three children, including a daughter who died during the first year of her life and who is the youngest of my Lenten companions. A degree of autobiography is included in some of the chapters to put things in context and to indicate why some of these companions have been so important to me at different stages in my life.

This is neither a traditional devotional book nor simply a series of biographies. Each companion provides a means of celebrating God's revelation of himself within ordinary human life. For those who may wish to use the book as an aid to more specific Lenten reflection, a passage of scripture is suggested which connects with the companion's story. A brief prayer concludes each chapter.

Each of my companions has died but all are still alive in my own life. Many sought to be faithful disciples of Jesus Christ. A few have been strangers to personal faith and religious commitment, but there has been something in them which has caused this believer to learn from them about the meaning of discipleship. Those of us who regularly worship often declare our belief in the Communion of Saints when reciting the Creed but too rarely see it as central to the practice of faith and discipleship.

The Communion of Saints is a glorious reminder that the Christian Church does not consist simply of those who are living now, but is a fellowship beyond space, time and geography. It is no dry doctrine. Experiencing its truth is exhilarating. In Susan Hill's novel *In the Springtime of the Year* a young widow is at worship in a village church.

> She became aware not of the presence of
> the village people sitting or kneeling behind
> her, but of others. The church was full
> of all those who'd ever prayed in it; the
> air was crammed and vibrating with their
> goodness and the freedom and power of

their resurrection, and she felt herself to
be part of some great living and growing
tapestry, every thread of which joined with
and crossed and belonged to every other,
though each one was also entirely and
distinctly itself.

A few of my companions would not have believed
in the Communion of Saints, or wanted to be in
a village church at all. But they are all part of my
personal pantheon. They have joined with and
crossed and belonged to each other through their
influence on me and what I believe and the person
I have become. They inhabit my prayers. Things
they have done, what they have said, poetry they
have written or art they have created – all provide a
living channel to God. Christianity is not an abstract
religion. The word of God became a human person,
who has fascinated the world for two millennia and
draws allegiance from billions today.

Christians are sometimes heard decrying celebrity
culture, but the term itself is a venerable one.
Celebrity emerges in late Middle English as a word
in common usage. It derives from the Latin *celeber*
and means *honoured*. In recent times the media has
tended to restrict celebrities to film stars, singers
and entertainers, with the Royal Family included

as honorary members of this elite. A few religious figures have gained celebrity status. Desmond Tutu, Pope John Paul II and Mother Teresa are obvious examples. John Paul II was certainly not averse to using the cult of celebrity to teach the Catholic faith and strengthen the Church by nurturing the bonds of affection for the Pope as the Vicar of Christ. His immediate successor was less comfortable in such a role, though he too knew that the Petrine office has a sprinkling of celebrity stardust to be used in the service of the Gospel. Pope Francis has quickly achieved celebrity status. Even Anglicans have got used to the Archbishop of Canterbury being given a media role and profile entirely out of keeping with the scale of his power and authority within the Church of England and the wider Anglican Communion. Justin Welby understands this and is not fazed by it.

The Christian faith has as its central figure someone born in obscurity who never travelled far and whose public ministry ended in judicial execution with only a few bystanders. This reminds us that those whom God honours, His celebrities, come from a much wider range of people than those who inhabit, whether willingly or not, celebrity magazines.

Blessed are the Pure in Heart
Charles Causley

Matthew 5.1–10

There are some people you feel you know even though you've never met them. The poet Charles Causley was one such person for me. He was Cornish through and through, even if those of us from west Cornwall consider Launceston (where he lived) a long way 'up country'.

At one level Charles Causley's life was very unadventurous. Apart from his student years and his war service he never lived anywhere other than Launceston. He taught until his early retirement in 1976 at the same school he had attended as a boy. He travelled widely in the summer holidays but continued living with his mother in her house. He was an only child.

Perhaps Causley's security in his life-setting was one of the reasons why he was able to stand apart from the mainstream of contemporary poetry. As a result he was one of England's underappreciated poets of the twentieth century. He owed little to the modernist movement. Causley's poems were inspired by ballads and popular folk songs. The novelist D. M. Thomas said of Causley, 'The surface simplicity of his style is deceptive. Many poets are simple while appearing to be profound. Causley, like Robert Frost, is the opposite'.

Read the 'The Ballad of the Bread Man' or 'Timothy Winters' and the meaning of Thomas's description of Causley's poetry becomes clear. The rhythm of these poems connects with some deep folk memory. You find yourself almost singing them as you read them. Causley's poetry is best heard, not simply read. The Bread Man is Jesus. The ballad recounts his birth, life and death. It is by turns funny, cheerful, tragic and profound. The Cornish cadences can be heard by those familiar with them. On the life of Jesus in Nazareth the poet says:

> When they got back to the village
> The neighbours said, to a man,
> 'That boy will never be one of us,
> Though he does what he blessed well can'.

And then a deep fear once held by ordinary working-class people is conjured – to be featured 'in the papers'. The culture of my Cornish childhood was the very opposite of the vision of Andy Warhol who suggested we would all seek 15 minutes of fame.

> He finished up in the papers
> He came to a very bad end,
> He was charged with bringing the living to
>   life.
> No man was that prisoner's friend.

The ballad ends with the Risen Christ offering loaves. 'Not today' they say as if to a travelling baker. The Bread of Life is rejected again.

By contrast, 'Timothy Winters' seems on the surface a secular poem. Timothy is a neglected child, perhaps representative of many Causley encountered. His clothes are tattered and his hair unkempt. 'A blitz of a boy is Timothy Winters'. The poem tells of his tragic life and its dire deprivations but then ends unexpectedly. Causley unashamedly uses a Cornish dialect word (helve), which refers to the sound of the distressed pleading of a cow when her calf is removed from her.

> At Morning Prayers the Master helves
> for children less fortunate than themselves

> and the loudest response in the room is
>   when
> Timothy Winters roars 'Amen!'
>
> So come one angel, come on ten
> Timothy Winters says 'Amen'
> Amen Amen Amen Amen.
> Timothy Winters, Lord. Amen.

A poem which begins with a vivid description of this 'blitz of a boy' concludes with the reader praying with and for him. How many clergy or teachers of prayer would envy an ability to draw people so subtly and confidently into praying? Yet Causley set out with no evangelistic intent. He lost his faith in his twenties and gradually regained it in middle age, though he was never any conventional churchman. He was so soaked in Christianity and its forms and imagery that his poetry is shaped by it, whether consciously or not.

When Charles Causley reached his 70th birthday many contemporary poets and writers contributed to a celebratory volume. Seamus Heaney, Ted Hughes, Elizabeth Jennings, Philip Larkin and Anthony Thwaite were among the honoured poets of their generation who did admire this unfashionable colleague and saw his greatness. Roger

McGough, whose own poetry is rather more in the Causley tradition, contributed two poems, one of which was the briefest of offerings.

> Causley, God, the sea:
> Cornish Trinity.

So much said and implied in so few words.

Mrs Causley had a stroke in 1966. She could still speak and use her left hand but was otherwise immobile. She needed full-time care. The general opinion was that as a bachelor and only child, Charles should put his mother in a long-term geriatric hospital. Everyone told him not to give up his teaching job. Even at the time he was convinced that if he had been a single woman he would have been expected to do the exact opposite.

As it turned out, a good friend came to the rescue and cared for Mrs Causley during the working day until Charles came home from school to look after her from 4pm onwards and overnight. His life was restricted. He talked to his mother about her own childhood. Poems flowed from his pen. As his own life became more constricted, his imagination was fed. The stream of poetry continued when her

11

decline was such that she needed hospitalization in her final years.

Causley's 'Ten Types of Hospital Visitor' was written from a depth of personal experience. Causley visited his mother regularly in her long last illness. He used free verse, a sign that he wasn't restricted to the rhythms of the ballad or folk song. That long poem provided me with insights into pastoral visiting entirely missing from my ordination training.

Charles Causley said of his mother, 'Her simple, Christian faith never wavered … she loved a church service and for seventy-five years had hardly missed a Sunday. On the other hand my feeling was that of Emerson: "I like the silent church before the service begins better than any preaching"'. When his mother died he had no difficulty in choosing her epitaph: 'Blessed are the pure in heart: for they shall see God'.

Charles Causley found himself a year after his mother's death in the Church of the Beatitudes in Galilee near where Jesus first preached the Sermon on the Mount. He wrote, 'There the words were again: "Blessed are the pure in heart: for they **shall** see God". Through the great window, I could see the Lake of Galilee: burning blue as the water in my mother's old, galvanized-iron wash tub, after she had put in the blue-bag on a childhood Monday in Cornwall, half a century before'.

The Bread Man, the Bread of Life and preacher of the Beatitudes never travelled far. He belonged to his locality so emphatically that we call him Jesus of Nazareth or the Man from Galilee. Charles Causley's mother never saw the Holy Land. She, like her son, belonged to Launceston, but the Galilean teacher was local to her, met by her in the scriptures, in her church, her prayers and her purity of heart. He was the source of her ability to see God.

Jesus of Nazareth, you never travelled far yet you were lifted up to draw the whole world to yourself; keep us mindful that the pure in heart are blessed and the meek will inherit the earth. Amen.

Vessels of Grace

Michael Stagg

2 Corinthians 4.7–12

It was touch and go whether the preacher for a special service in Norwich Cathedral in July 2011 would be well enough to make it. Michael Stagg had been diagnosed with cancer and the prognosis was not good. The service was a biennial one for retired clergy, widows and widowers followed by lunch in the grounds of Bishop's House. Michael did make it and preached a sermon never to be forgotten. He produced a glazed pot and from the elevated pulpit threw it on the sanctuary floor where it smashed into smithereens. The senior clergy sitting below nearly jumped out of their cassocks. He provided a vivid reminder of St Paul's words: 'We are no better than pots of earthenware to contain this treasure' (2 Corinthians 4.7). The treasure is the Gospel. The pots of earthenware are human beings. We are fragile, cracked and misshapen yet God chooses us to be vessels of his grace, and even calls some of us to be ministers of his words and sacraments. The cracked pot called Michael Stagg certainly contained the treasure of the Gospel in and through his humanity. He was immensely treasured. Just over a year later the cathedral was packed for his funeral requiem.

Michael Hubert Stagg was born just as the Second World War broke out. He trained for ordination at St Chad's College, Durham, before exercising a ministry in several dioceses as a parish priest, bishop's chaplain and diocesan communications officer. It wasn't a ministry of glittering prizes. Michael himself told me that he had often seen congregations decline. He never rated himself much of a success as a parish priest. So why the full cathedral when he died at the age of 72, several years into his retirement?

Michael's estimate of himself and his ministry was often downplayed. He was a great parish priest but some elements of a vicar's job did not always play to his strengths. Strategic leadership and business administration didn't excite him. Contemplative prayer, leading retreats, spiritual direction, leading people to God through friendship and conversation: in these he excelled. Those who did fall within his care cherished Michael enormously. He exercised a very personal ministry. That creates its own limitation, organizationally and numerically. The seven years of Michael's retirement were some of the happiest in his whole ministry. Freed from parochial structures, his wider ministry as a spiritual director took off. Clergy and lay people alike sought him out. Michael was often the first to tell me of pastoral need or of someone for whom I ought to pray. He read voraciously and had an intensely enquiring theological mind. He also had a great sense of humour.

Michael was my predecessor's chaplain and diocesan communications officer, appointed in 1989. A couple of years later, the *Eastern Daily Press* reported that two nuns from Ditchingham, Sr Louise and Sr Rebecca, had kidnapped Michael as part of that year's Comic Relief Appeal. The sisters looked resplendent in their habits topped off with red noses and masks. They took Michael to the Bishop with a ransom demand. According to the *Eastern Daily Press*, Michael commented at the time, 'It was dreadful. It turned out I was only worth a couple of quid'.

Michael knew that being named after an archangel was dangerous. It's a name hard to live up to. It means 'Who is like unto God?' In the Revelation of St John the Divine, Michael is the warrior fighting the heavenly battle against the dragon, the devil to be cast with the bad angels into destruction. In some apocryphal Christian literature, Michael becomes a central figure. In the Testament of Abraham, for example, Michael's prayers of intercession are so powerful they can even rescue souls from hell. It was that tradition which led to Michael the Archangel being invoked for the care of the sick in the Eastern Church. The cult spread, which is why there are so many churches and hospitals dedicated to St Michael in Western Europe, including England.

Michael Stagg certainly prayed for people. He had an astonishing ministry of intercession. He remembered birthdays and anniversaries and surprised many by such commemoration of them. His intercessions informed his pastoral ministry. The two were never separate for Michael. You couldn't care for people if you didn't pray for them. If you didn't pray for them you wouldn't care for them. Michael was aptly named.

He never drew attention to his second name, Hubert, and may not have been very fond of it. St Hubert was the Bishop of Maastricht and died in the early eighth century long before the Maastricht Treaty caused John Major's government such trouble. We don't know much for certain about St Hubert's life since there are scant contemporary records. But a later story tells of his conversion to Christianity as a young man while out hunting one Good Friday. It's said that Hubert saw an image of the crucified Christ between the antlers of a stag. The vision of the cross of Christ captured his mind and soul. His life was transformed. Paintings of St Hubert, including one in the National Gallery, include a stag as an emblem. No second name could have been more appropriate for Michael Stagg, though he could hardly be described as a huntsman. Like Hubert his namesake, he was drawn to the Cross. His gaze was fixed on it, as was his life.

When visiting Michael in hospital I mentioned to him the journal of Philip Toynbee (another companion in this book). Michael knew of it, as I thought he would, since he seemed to have read almost everything. When Philip was lying in hospital and thinking about the Cross, he once wrote that 'the community of pain is the community of love'. Michael understood that too, never more so than in his final illness. He knew too that not all suffering in this world is caused by disease or sin or hatred. A lot of suffering is caused by love. Someone you love can hurt you deeply by the things they say or do. A betrayed lover can become disconsolate. Even when the relationship is one of great mutuality, there is the enormous pain which comes with grief and bereavement. Love brings suffering. The Cross of Christ speaks of this mysterious connection between God's love and Christ's willingness to suffer with and for us. Michael saw all life through that refraction.

I last saw Michael before going off to attend a residential meeting of the House of Bishops a few days before he died. He wanted to know what we were going to talk about so that he could pray for us. There was nothing affected about it. Michael was too sharp to be spiritually cloying. But he wanted to be alive and connected to the very end. In that last encounter I asked for Michael's blessing. The last words he said to me on earth were words of prayer for me, my family and my ministry.

'We are no better than pots of earthenware to contain this treasure'. St Paul was right. In Michael Stagg those who knew him saw one of those pots shining with the lustre which comes from the glazing of Christ the master potter. Jesus Christ took the clay that was Michael Stagg and made from him a bright vessel of grace.

> *Christ the master potter, mould us according to your design that we may be adequate vessels of your grace with lives fashioned in obedience to your service. Amen.*

3

The Vulnerability of Love

John Miller

Colossians 1.15–20

Imet John Miller initially when he became one of the first lay canons of Truro Cathedral in 1993. At one time John thought about testing his vocation to the religious life, but his vocation was to be as an artist painting landscapes and seascapes, especially the beaches of west Cornwall. He joined the Third Order of the Society of St Francis, and St Francis of Assisi's capacity to see God's presence in every detail of the created order shaped John Miller's spirituality as well. As with St Francis, the Cross of Christ had a central place in John's faith too. He lived faithfully within the disciplines of the Church of England, smiling at its foibles and eccentricities, irritated by its idiocies, but warm in his affection for the verities and continuities it represented.

John was not a preacher (though his paintings were a proclamation of faith in their own way), but he was once persuaded into the pulpit of Truro Cathedral. It was when Craigie Aitchison's paintings on four previously blank panels behind the altar in St Margaret's Chapel were dedicated. Each panel depicts the crucifixion in typical Aitchison style. Like John Miller, Aitchison was a great colourist and struck out a path for himself in twentieth-century British art, belonging to no easily defined school. Aitchison's crucifixions often depict Christ on the Cross against highly coloured backgrounds. The Cross looks lonely and isolated, the very effect Aitchison intended. He was not a great churchgoer but became fascinated by the crucifixion which he described as the most horrific story he had ever heard. He said that as long as the world existed one should attempt to record it.

John Miller's paintings are much gentler, almost pastoral. He was not drawn to paint the crucifixion again and again as Aitchison did, but the redemptive character of what Christ had done for humankind was personally significant to him. It was because of the Cross and Christ's resurrection that John did not see the world as ultimately tragic but one which was redeemed and so to be celebrated in all its richness and diversity.

John Miller was born in 1931. His father was an architect with London County Council. The family

sent John to St Joseph's College, Beulah Hill, a
Roman Catholic boys' school run by the De la Salle
Brothers (the school continues to this day, joined
the state system in 1972 and is now an academy).
John's parents were not Roman Catholics but an
uncle had been educated there and the school had
a good reputation. While many people recall bad
experiences of their education in such establish-
ments, John's recollections were very different. He
believed he was shown a set of values for life. He
was impressed by the way the brothers lived by such
a rigorous timetable, rising at 5.30 a.m. and praying
the monastic offices throughout the day as well as
teaching. He observed that 'it was a severe life for
them but they were not severe with the pupils'.

John was fascinated by the spirituality which
surrounded him. One of the brothers encouraged
him to explore Christian mystics such as St John of
the Cross, St Teresa of Avila and Julian of Norwich.
Somehow it was as if the spirituality latent within him
had been given fresh air and he commented that 'once
that part of oneself has been enlivened it can never be
put back to sleep'. He began to experience what he
believed to be the unity of time and space in God.

All this happened against the background of war.
John was a messenger boy for the ARP (Air Raid

Precautions) wardens. He and other adolescent boys in London were sent off on bicycles in tin hats to incidents where their task was to keep the wardens and rescue workers on site in touch with the central ARP post. So he found himself in the early years of adolescence assisting in extricating the dead and injured from bombed buildings. He recalled that 'on one occasion I threw down my bicycle and leaped behind a low garden wall to avoid the bullets from a Heinkel bomber which was spraying the street as it passed over only two or three hundred feet above the ground. It left a United Dairies' horse dead in the shafts and several people badly injured and dead in its wake including children'.

John's education did not come merely from the school but from these experiences too. He recognized that he had seen good and evil, things which caused him delight as well as things which confused him. His conviction even then was that everything in the world 'has gathered into a ball of light which I knew at once to be absolute love'.

The images of the Belsen concentration camp made a big impact upon John when he watched them with his father on a visit to the cinema. In response, John felt he needed to give his life to a sacred cause as part of the atonement of the world for such sin.

Rather wisely his father insisted he should delay any decision about becoming a Roman Catholic and testing his vocation. In the meantime John went to art school and worked in the theatre before being called up for National Service. He was sent to Malta. During an exercise he sustained some serious injuries which led to months in a military hospital where he came very near to death. This realization prompted John to celebrate even more keenly the good things in life he had taken for granted. As he recovered, his bed was placed on a balcony from which he could look across the valley at the beautiful architecture of Mdina. He began to paint and had the time to explore the use of colour, light and space. His vocation in life became clear to him.

After the war, John worked for a firm of church architects, helping to design some of the buildings at the Anglican shrine of Our Lady of Walsingham. There he met Michael Truscott, who was also thinking of becoming a monk. Their common yearning for a lively spiritual life was the foundation of a partnership which lasted until John's death. It was as a church architect that John first came to west Cornwall to examine the rood screen at St Buryan. Soon afterwards Michael and John opened a guest house not far from Land's End and in 1960 John had his first public exhibition of his art in

Penzance. The trajectory of his career was set as well as the pattern of his life.

On at least one occasion John extended his artistic range by creating a crucifix. This was for the chapel at St Michael's Mount. Lord and Lady St Levan, who lived there, wanted to restore the chapel to its medieval simplicity but found it hard to find a suitable crucifix. John offered to craft one himself and the offer was immediately accepted. As he tried to shape a suitable figure in clay suspended on wire hung from three nails he found it a more challenging commission than he expected. One night the figure collapsed, leaving the arms rather more elongated and outstretched than intended. Looking at it afresh, John saw in the figure a welcoming embrace and knew that this was how the figure had to be. He wrote of the experience: 'As I worked on the final carving I contemplated the terrible death by crucifixion. I recalled a man from Auschwitz concentration camp saying "after so much suffering how could one depict the suffering of one man". I knew then I had to try to show the vulnerability of absolute love over and above pain'. As John wrote and painted, so he lived.

> *God of unity, in the glory of your world*
> *we discern your creative power; deepen our*

*appreciation that your love for all you have
made is unquenchable despite the suffering we
endure. Amen.*

4

Resisting Temptation
Stanley Green

Luke 4.1–13

I only knew his name after he died. Stanley Green had obituaries in the *Daily Telegraph*, *The Times* and *The Guardian* following his death in January 1994. He had become one of London's eccentrics, a sight to be pointed out as he carried his placards up and down Oxford Street selling home produced booklets warning everyone to eat less protein.

I recall first seeing him on a visit to London towards the end of the 1970s. He was a human billboard. His homemade placard had so much writing on it that from a distance I could not decipher it. I assumed he was telling us that 'The end of the world is nigh' and that we should 'Repent of our sins and flee the wrath to come'. I even pulled my scarf around my clerical collar so that I wouldn't be identified with him when I got nearer.

As it was, his message wasn't religious at all, though it was pursued with evangelistic fervour. He was a crusading vegetarian, though of a very particular kind. Stanley Green believed that we ate too much protein and that this, together with sitting down too often, caused people to store uncontrollable amounts of passion which led to an overflow of lust.

He advocated 'protein wisdom'. A reduced intake of protein would, he argued, make for healthier, happier and kinder people. During his period of service with the Royal Navy, the obsession of his fellow sailors with sex caused him to develop his theories. He was shocked by the way their passions seemed to be so uncontrolled. He sought to avoid lust and to maintain coolness of judgement by eating porridge, apples, pulses and bread which he made himself. 'Passion can be a great torment' he claimed. His one-man campaign was a six-day-a-week job, based in Oxford Street. He commuted from a council flat in Northolt, and gave his life entirely to his protein mission from 1968, the year after his parents had both died within 12 months of each other. Whether bereavement led to the single mindedness with which he gave himself to his cause is impossible to judge. Stanley Green gave away little of his inner life, despite becoming a London character who was interviewed by various newspapers and magazines. He is the only human billboard to rate an entry in the *Oxford Dictionary of National Biography*.

Stanley had a series of unskilled jobs before becoming a self-employed gardener while continuing to live with his parents in their final years. He was 53 when he gave up paid employment to devote himself entirely to his cause. His booklets explaining 'protein wisdom' were self-printed on ancient machinery he kept in his flat. The Museum of London possesses copies of his pamphlets, printed with a peculiar disregard for punctuation, capital letters and consistent typesetting.

I saw Stanley Green frequently when we lived in London. Most people ignored him, though he claimed to have sold 87,000 copies of the booklets over the years. Some found Stanley disturbing and a few thought he was threatening. He was twice arrested for public obstruction. He could get into altercations, particularly with young women when he told them they would not be able to deceive their husbands into believing they were virgins on their wedding night. He was largely oblivious to changed sexual mores and expectations. He wore overalls since he was often spat at, appearing to accept such ill treatment with remarkable equanimity. He had

no religious faith but he did claim to say a prayer –
'quite a good prayer, unselfish too' – before retiring
to bed each night, 'a sort of acknowledgement of
God, just in case there happens to be one'.

Stanley Green made few, if any, disciples, and
his 'protein wisdom' died with him. I came to
admire his solitary dedication, self-determination
and eccentricity. He was strangely unbothered by
what other people made of him, and yet continued
to want to engage with everyone he met. He was
a man with a mission, not discouraged by lack of
converts, but not embittered either.

The oddness of any encounter with Stanley
prompted me to reflect on the many eccentrics in
the Bible and in later Christian history. John the
Baptist, with his diet of locusts and wild honey,
may not have practised 'protein wisdom' but lived
a solitary life on the edge of society, even if people
were much more attracted to him than they were to
Stanley Green.

To be eccentric simply means being 'off centre'.
Even Jesus was that, inhabiting the rural fringes of
Galilean society. The most populous town in his
part of Galilee, Sepphoris, doesn't rate a mention
in the New Testament. It seems possible that Jesus

never went there, preferring the smaller villages and the countryside.

In contemporary Western society, Christians often feel off centre. Looking at the world from the perspective of faith appears increasingly eccentric. But being off centre has advantages. You often see things more clearly from an angle. The best portrait photographs are rarely taken with the face directly to camera. Seen in profile, the human face is more revealing. You seem to look more directly into someone's character.

Eccentrics know the isolation of being misunderstood, mocked, thought gullible and unintelligent. That's been the experience of many whom the Church has called saints down the ages. Eccentricity and sanctity are often found together.

The instinct of most Anglicans is to work with the grain of society, to be part of the mainstream and not to stand uncomfortably at the edge or be marginal to it. It's a dangerous vocation since it can lead to an unthinking validation of whatever may be the social conventions of the time. That's why figures such as Stanley Green, eccentric though they are, remind us that conviction and, yes, passion (even though he did not like the word himself) are sometimes solitary experiences. John the Baptist knew that. So did Jesus in the wilderness, where solitariness made temptation greater. And where Jesus resisted the temptation to be like everyone else.

> *God of the rejected, look upon those of us*
> *eccentric enough to believe in you and your*
> *love and mercy; help us resist the temptation*
> *to be like everyone else and give us confidence*
> *in our convictions. Amen.*

5

Transforming Love
Monica Furlong

Mark 12.28–34

In 1975, the year of my ordination as a deacon, I bought a small paperback book. It was Monica Furlong's *Christian Uncertainties*. Newly minted as an Anglo Catholic curate, I was a mixture of liberal theology and conservative Catholicism. On a council estate in Peterborough I would refer in sermons to 'the author of the Fourth Gospel' rather than St John. I did not want to mislead. I would explain how Matthew, Mark and Luke had a purpose in composing their narratives. The scriptures were a happy hunting ground of puzzles to be solved. My diocesan bishop got to hear of an early sermon on 'the abomination of desolation' (Mark 13). Bishop Douglas Feaver (he features elsewhere in this book) had already instructed me not to preach from the newspapers but from the scriptures. So he then approved of me. (It didn't last.)

I may have been theologically liberal but at that stage I was opposed to the further marriage of the divorced in church, the ordination of women to the priesthood, communion before confirmation and almost any of the pending reforms to catholic order which I could see looming over the horizon. While some evangelicals believed the scriptures to be inerrant, I placed my trust in an unchanging Church (though in truth I knew it had changed a lot). It was an emotional rather than an intellectual response.

At the time, Monica Furlong wrote regular short articles in the *Church Times*, eventually published in the small book I bought. Some of them I still remember nearly 40 years later. One was about 'love of neighbour'. I read it just after returning from our church youth club. The curate was inevitably in charge. I didn't really want to spend every Sunday evening with young people but felt bad about not much wanting to do so. After all, wasn't I ordained because I wanted to be of help to others, to bring them on in the Christian life? How could you do that if you didn't always feel a natural interest in them? What made it worse was hearing people say how good the new curate was with the young. Was it all an act?

Monica Furlong confessed that she thought she was worse at loving her neighbour than almost anyone she had ever known. She said that she only felt completely at ease with two kinds of people – those who knew her well and those who didn't know her at all. It was the kind of partial knowledge of another person often included in the term 'neighbour' which she found to be the most difficult of all relationships. Whenever she was told that Christians should be perpetually open to the needs of the stranger she felt that her personality was simply not extrovert enough for the demands of the Gospel. Her understanding of loving her neighbour required a deliberate choice sometimes not to be with other people, enabling solitude to provide the sort of inner space necessary for growth. She noticed that scholars, artists and musicians can only give themselves to others if quite long periods of their lives are spent alone and without continual interruption.

I understood at once what she meant. It came as a liberation. By then I had come to know some of our religious communities. The sisters I knew did seem to love their neighbour. But they were not frantic to be with their neighbours all the time. They needed to cultivate their inner space. Love of God, neighbour and oneself were a trinity, with the mutuality and distinction characteristic of our Trinitarian God.

It was because Monica Furlong was able to address my spiritual experience that I found what she wrote about marriage and divorce, the place of women in the Church or abortion so challenging. I have re-read *Christian Uncertainties* and now wonder what disturbed me since things have moved on so far. It was Monica Furlong, and then Wendy Perriam's novels, which caused me to tone down some of my early sermons on the Blessed Virgin Mary in which she was idealized out of flesh and blood existence. And perhaps Monica was more prescient than she knew when she expressed a fear that when women were ordained (as she believed was bound to happen) they 'might become a carbon copy of the priests that we already have, and I would like to see something different evolve'. Women have not only been priests but have fulfilled established roles as rectors, vicars, canons and deans. I wonder if Monica would now think our female clergy have been allowed or have dared enough to be different.

Monica Furlong could get things wrong. Re-reading what she had to say nearly 40 years ago about pornography, I realize that she was writing in reaction to the heyday of Mary Whitehouse and her campaign to clean up television. Monica suggested that the best Christian reaction to pornography was to laugh at it. I understand what she meant. But the contemporary experience of pornography and its violence against women makes me now more sympathetic to Mrs Whitehouse than I ever was at the time. I met Monica Furlong when she was writing an affectionate but critical book about the Church of England in the 1990s. She represented the very best tradition of the intellectually questioning Anglican, committed to the Church of England but always in critical solidarity with it. Had she been born a generation later she might well have been ordained herself, but would perhaps have lost the critical edge and freedom she possessed if she had been.

Monica's father was a Catholic, though gradually ceased to practise since Monica's mother was caustic about religion. Monica found faith for herself. She knew what it was to have a conversion experience. She wrote about it. It was an experience of the love of God unmediated by preacher, priest or scriptures:

> "I sat in the grounds of Lincoln's Inn one
> bright August day, sad and frightened by
> life and by myself … The sun had gone
> behind a cloud, and behind the greyness

there was a dazzling radiance that I felt
might have blinded me if I had seen it in
full. A huge inner contraction took place,
an excruciating bringing to birth, and then
I knew myself loved, accepted, forgiven,
laughed at, laughed with, touched,
held, set free. It was the most important
moment since I was born."

Monica translated this experience into a Christian life lived within the Church of England. Joost de Blank, a Dutch Anglican priest of wide culture and experience (later Bishop of Stepney and Archbishop of Cape Town), helped her see 'organised religion as the container that sheltered us from, but also held us within, the hands of the living God'.

Monica would have been well used to the recitation of the Summary of the Law at the Eucharist. In Mark's Gospel, it is a lawyer who asks Jesus 'which commandment is first of all?' The answer always connected Monica with her experience at Lincoln's Inn.

Jesus quotes Deuteronomy 6.4–5, a statement of faith about the unity of God and the need to love him with heart, soul, mind and strength. He then adds Leviticus 19.18 ('Love your neighbour as yourself"). It is possible that Jesus was not being entirely original, though as far as I know we have no evidence that any other Jewish teacher combined these two commands. What Jesus says suggests that these injunctions are not simply the way in which the rest of the law is validated but so fundamental that the detailed provisions of other laws cannot be as important. To love God and to love your neighbour as yourself 'is more important than all burnt offerings and sacrifices' the lawyer then says to Jesus. To which Jesus replies, 'you are not far from the Kingdom of God'. That's as firm a validation as anyone ever received from Jesus himself. It was gospel music to the ears of Monica Furlong.

God of light and love, visit us with your transforming radiance in our daily lives, and enable us to love you and our neighbours as ourselves. Amen.

6

Prophets with Honour

Lionel James

Mark 6.1–6

In Cornwall in 1932 a young man, a surface labourer on a tin mine, had candidated for the Wesleyan Methodist ministry. He came from an unchurched family and had found faith in his local chapel, Pool Wesley. His parents took little interest. The only encouragement he received was from his maternal grandmother who could neither read nor write. She was immensely proud of her grandson.

This is the story of my father, Lionel James. The year 1932 was that of Methodist Church union. The Wesleyans, the Primitive Methodists and the United Methodist Church all came together to form the Methodist Church as we know it today. The new Church found itself with a surplus of 200 ministers. Too many candidates for ordination were in the pipeline. Seventy men received an identical letter terminating their candidature, and my father was one of them. The letter declared he had the gifts and graces for Christian ministry but circumstances prevented him entering training that year. In 1932 Lionel was 25. That was then the upper age limit for candidates for ordination, as it remained in Methodism until after the Second World War. He would be too old in 1933.

It was a devastating letter for Lionel to receive. But his parents were pleased. They thought their son was growing away from them, and getting ideas above his station.

Lionel decided to enrol at the local School of Mines to study for a diploma in mining engineering. It took him five years to complete, walking several miles to his classes after work each day on the mine. The diploma was a passport to a better life. By now he was in his early 30s though he still lived at home. He had been engaged for more than eight years to my mother, whom he met at his chapel. She came from a committed Methodist family and worked as a shop assistant. The two of them were so poor that marriage seemed impossible, but if he got a job as a mining engineer and moved away from Cornwall new possibilities would open up.

On the evening he was due to receive his diploma

at what was as grand a ceremony as the School of Mines could put on, my grandparents told Lionel they wouldn't come. They could not understand why he was not satisfied with his life as it was. They took offence at his desire to better himself. He needed to be kept in his place. 'Jesus said to them, "prophets are not without honour, except in their home town, and among their own kin, and in their own house"' (Mark 6.3, 4).

Those words in the scriptures meant more to Lionel than almost any other. It was not simply his parents who did not understand. It was those with whom he worked and neighbours in his street. They thought he reckoned himself superior to them, though truly he didn't. He wanted to tell people of the love of God in Jesus Christ which he had found. It was this which meant he wanted to use such gifts as God had given him. The diploma in mining engineering would have mattered little to him if he could have trained for ordination. When he read in the gospel that Jesus could do no deed of power in his home town he understood. He often felt that he couldn't preach quite so well in his home chapel or gain the same response as he did when he went elsewhere. His heart was almost broken by his own family. 'And he was amazed at their unbelief' it says of Jesus about those among whom he lived.

My parents eventually married in April 1939 and moved to London since my father had gained a job as a mineral analyst. It did not last long, since he was now in a reserved occupation. When war broke out he and my mother were sent to north Wales where Lionel worked secretly in an underground bunker on the development of chemical weapons. Many of the locals thought they were war dodgers so there was no respite from disapproval.

Lionel's vocation to be a minister of word and sacrament never left him. After the war he discovered it was possible in Congregationalism to take on a small church and study for the examinations of the Congregational Union of England and Wales while doing so. So he did, though he was never really a Congregationalist in his heart. He served in Torrington at the time of my birth, moving to Newquay in 1952. The Congregational Church there grew steadily under his leadership. He became much more sacramental in outlook, and decided in 1961 that he must offer for ordination in the Church of England. At the age of 54 he found himself at Queen's College, Birmingham, and was ordained to a curacy in Northampton. He had been one of the best paid Congregational ministers in south-west England, and took a cut of more than half his stipend to become an Anglican curate. He was a man of conviction. My mother was something of a saint to cope with it all.

I told some of the story of my father's life and ministry in a sermon for the annual Festival of The Corporation of the Friends and Sons of the Clergy at St Paul's Cathedral. When my parents finally retired in 1974 the Corporation bought them a retirement bungalow in which they lived for more than 25 years, the longest they remained anywhere. Somewhere in the archives of the Corporation are repeated letters of gratitude from my father. He was overwhelmed by this kindness. He knew how to do gratitude well, having received so little of it in his early life.

We often appreciate our parents more the older we get. I reflect nowadays upon my father's vocational resilience. Often isolated from his family, without the close fellowship of his Methodist chapel and especially his class meeting (the genius of Methodism) his vocation would not have survived. Nor would mine without the church communities of which I have been part, my own family who have travelled with me, and fellow students at university long ago who helped shape my faith. Solidarity within a shared episcopate has been important too. We do not minister alone, but as members one of another in the body of Christ, the One Holy, Catholic and Apostolic Church.

My own vocational journey has been easy compared with my father's. Yet I notice that some newly ordained clergy are surprised by the toughness of parochial ministry. I begin to wonder whether the affirming culture of our present Church, and our tendency to go overboard with delight about young vocations, always serves young Christian ministers well. We invite those about to be ordained to say where and in what context they want to serve. We even enquire of them what sort of house they need and how many bedrooms. Have we minimized the sacrifice of vocation too much? We do not want clergy to have financial and other worries which can be a distraction from mission and ministry, but equally we should not attempt to remove sacrifice and self-offering from vocation to ministry. They are essential.

St Paul says in his letter to the Philippians that Jesus, being in the form of God, did not regard equality with God as something to be exploited but 'emptied himself taking the form of a slave, being born in human likeness'. Such is the sacrifice of vocation. For my father it was imposed on him. For many of us the challenges of ministry and its disappointments remind us just how much we have to learn about self-giving if we are to serve Christ. Jesus Christ is discovered in weakness, the weakness of the Saviour on the Cross, dying that we may live. Prophets are not without honour, certainly. But priests are not made without sacrifice.

> *Lord Jesus, you knew the pain of rejection*
> *in your own country and among your own*
> *people; empower those who follow your call to*
> *bear misunderstanding and hostility and to*
> *share in your sacrifice. Amen.*

7

The Scandal of the Incarnation
John Everett Millais

Luke 2.41–52

When we lived in central London we used to go to the Tate Gallery, now Tate Britain, quite often. I found I wanted to revisit paintings more often than I wanted to see new ones. The painting which caught my attention most in those days was John Everett Millais' *Christ in the House of His Parents*.

It was painted in 1849 when Millais was just 20 years old. He was one of the founders of the Pre-Raphaelite Brotherhood, along with Holman Hunt and Dante Gabriel Rossetti, also very young men. They were doing something modern and daring, yet thought of themselves as recreating an artistic tradition which pre-dated the time of Raphael (who died in 1520). They believed in perfect likenesses of the human form. Landscape should be minutely observed. Costumes should be faithful to the period. They wanted to recreate what they believed was natural.

Millais' painting of Christ created a sensation when shown at the Royal Academy in its 1850 exhibition. It caused outrage, and was condemned on both artistic and religious grounds. The painting was inspired by a sermon Millais heard in Oxford in 1849. It shows Jesus as a young boy. He is in Joseph's workshop. The tools of the carpenter's trade are on display and there are wood shavings all over the floor. Mary kneels beside Jesus and the picture captures a moment when they are on the brink of a warm embrace. Jesus has just cut himself. Blood pours from his hand. There has been some sort of accident. Was he experimenting with his father's tools when Joseph's back was turned? Who knows? It is a painting of realistic intimacy. It verges on the sentimental, but is saved from such a judgement by the richness of its symbolism.

The love of Mary for her son is precisely that of any parent seeking to comfort, strengthen and support her hurting child. Joseph stands a little apart, hands outstretched towards Jesus, concerned but uncertain what to do. He is like many fathers when such domestic incidents take place. It is Mary who is closest to Jesus. It is to his mother that the boy turns.

In Millais' painting the carpenter's shop is linked with the passion of Christ since the boy's wounded hand and the blood which has dripped onto his left foot prefigure his later wounds on the Cross. A young John the Baptist carries a bowl of water towards his cousin, anticipating Christ's baptism. The way in which Mary kneels beside her son heralds an even greater tragedy when he is nailed to a Cross before which she will also kneel, her heart broken.

Millais lived in Oxford, at the heart of the Tractarian movement. John Henry Newman had converted to Roman Catholicism only five years before Millais' painting was first publicly displayed. Millais would paint a famous portrait of Newman late in life in 1881, by which time they were both great national figures. Some of the critics thought they saw the influence of the Oxford Movement within the painting, not least in the central place given to Mary. While in London, Millais attended St Andrew's, Wells Street, built in 1847 and one of the most advanced high Anglican churches at the time. He studiously avoided comment on any connection between his faith, the Oxford Movement and the painting. As he grew older he said less and less about any religious convictions he held. Millais, a churchgoer as a young man, ceased to go to church much at all in mid-Victorian England. Nonetheless he became one of England's most favoured artists as his style gradually became more conventional. He ended up as a pillar of the establishment and President of the Royal Academy. The reception *Christ in the House of his Parents* received may account for a good deal of his religious reticence since it was condemned in the pages of the most honoured national newspapers as well as by Victorian England's most eminent novelist.

The Times, in an age when it discussed high art in its editorials, described Millais' painting as revolting and disgusting. But this was mild compared with the rant Charles Dickens published in June 1850. He was scarcely known as an art critic and nor was he a fervent churchgoer. But he had an image of the Holy Family in his mind which Millais' painting offended. He wrote:

> "In the foreground of that carpenter's shop
> is a hideous, blubbering, red headed boy in
> a bed gown; who appears to have received a
> poke in the hand, from the stick of another
> boy with whom he has been playing in an
> adjacent gutter, and to be holding it up for
> the contemplation of a kneeling woman,
> so horrible in her ugliness that she would

stand out from the rest of the company as
a monster in the vilest cabaret in France,
or the lowest gin shop in England. Two
almost naked carpenters, master and
journeyman, worthy companions of this
agreeable female, are working at their trade;
a boy, with some small flavour of humanity
in him, is entering with a vessel of water;
and nobody is paying any attention to
a snuffy old woman who seems to have
mistaken that shop for the tobacconist next
door and to be hopelessly waiting at the
counter to be served with half an ounce of
her favourite mixture."

It is strange that Dickens should hate the realism of
such a painting when his own novels depicted the
realism of the squalor of life in London so vividly.
Millais tended to avoid religious subjects for his
later art, and never again focused on Christ himself.

In 1850 the Roman Catholic hierarchy had just been
restored in England. Despite Newman's conversion
to Roman Catholicism, the Oxford Movement in
the Church of England was growing in strength
and Protestants were alarmed. Even if *Christ in the
House of his Parents* did not win immediate approval,
a lot of the Pre-Raphaelites' other work did. Queen

Victoria was sufficiently interested to ask to see Millais' painting in private. No record exists of what she made of it although Millais himself said he hoped it would have no bad effects on her mind.

Despite all this, it is hard not to give some of the credit for the controversy to the scandal of the incarnation itself. Millais had reminded everyone that Jesus Christ, Saviour and Lord, was once a young child who would cry when he hurt himself and who would want his mother. The strong, majestic Christ of saving power in the Protestant tradition was not often seen at the time in the weakness of a child. Charles Dickens, who, just a year or two before his attack on Millais, had written a small unpublished book for his children about Christ, depicted him less as Saviour and Incarnate Lord than as comforting moral teacher. His blistering attack on Millais' painting seems aimed almost unconsciously at the shocking idea that God should become incarnate.

We are less likely to be affronted now by a painting of Jesus, after a childhood accident, showing his vulnerability. But the scandal of the incarnation remains. That God should come and live among us as one of us is beyond our capacity to understand. Are we unshocked nowadays by Millais' painting because we understand what he was seeking to convey? Or is it because our belief in the incarnation is so much weaker, and among many entirely rejected? Despite being someone whose own faith is so elusive, Millais still presents a challenge to us across the generations.

Scandalous God, you affront us by sending your Son Jesus Christ to live among us; forgive our incapacity to comprehend your incarnate love, seen in the carpenter's shop at Nazareth and fully revealed on the Cross of Calvary. Amen.

8

Blessed are the Poor
Eva Peron

Luke 6.20–26

On 26 July 1952 all radio programmes in Argentina were interrupted with a solemn announcement: 'The Sub-Secretariat of Information fulfils the very sad duty of announcing that at 8.25 p.m. this evening Senora Eva Peron, the spiritual leader of the nation, passed away'.

The 'spiritual leader of the nation' was just 33 years old, the same age, as some noted at the time, as Jesus Christ when he was crucified. For many in Argentina it did seem like the death of their saviour. Immediately Buenos Aires fell silent and dark. It was originally intended that Eva's body would lie in state for three days. Crowds too large to count kept coming. A fortnight passed before her lying in state came to an end, caused only by the fact that her body needed fresh embalming.

Her funeral was one of the biggest anywhere in the world in the twentieth century. Only Diana, Princess of Wales, and Pope John Paul II had funerals which matched it. But Eva Peron had only been in the public eye for six or seven years. She was born in poverty, an illegitimate child. A decade before her death she was an unsuccessful bit-part actress who scarcely earned enough to feed herself. Her story is remarkable and contested. For many in Argentina she was a saint. For others she was no better than a common prostitute.

I became hooked on her story through Andrew Lloyd Webber and Tim Rice's musical, *Evita*. Several visits to Buenos Aires have deepened that fascination further. In 2007 I took my wife to Buenos Aires for the first time. We walked through the customs building on arrival past an official in a booth who had two postcards on the wall behind him. One was of the Virgin Mary. The other was of Eva Peron. It spoke volumes. More recently Eva's portrait has been set up in lights on the tower of the old Ministry of Public Works. She presides over Buenos Aires, especially at night.

Eva was born in May 1919 in Los Toldos, a pampas settlement about 150 miles west of Buenos Aires. She was her mother's fifth and final illegitimate child. Eva Maria, as she was baptized, always used her father's surname, Duarte, but it's unlikely she had any real memory of him. Juan Duarte lived 20 miles away where he had a wife and family. He worked regularly in Los Toldos and for months at a time lived with Eva's mother. After his long-term work in Los Toldos came to an end he left his mistress and her five children to fend entirely for themselves.

Eva was just six when her father died. Her mother took her children to the funeral. They were unwelcome, unsurprisingly. The searing injustice of it all must have made a huge impression on this young child. She knew poverty but experienced social stigma too.

Most girls like Eva would have expected to marry a local man, have children and continue the cycle of poverty. Something in Eva (was it resentment, courage or a sense of adventure?) led her to relocate to Buenos Aires at the age of 15.

The usual explanation is that she became the mistress of a tango singer called Agustin Magaldi when he came to perform in her locality. *Evita*, the musical, presents this story as fact. As it is, there's no evidence that Agustin Magaldi performed anywhere near Los Toldos. In any case he always took his wife, and often his mother, on his tours. He was a very unlikely lothario.

The less spectacular explanation is that Eva's mother took her to Buenos Aires where her young daughter was determined to make her way as an actress. Her opponents said she slept her way to the small parts she got but it's likely she was as much sinned against as sinning. Theatrical producers did not regard young women like Eva with honour.

She made herself useful to those running a movie magazine, having discovered that journalists liked stories brought to them. Then she started to organize other actors and actresses to perform plays on the expanding radio stations of Argentina. She proved a highly competent organizer. She kept the leading parts in these radio plays for herself. Her voice became well known.

In early 1944 she met Juan Peron, Minister of Labour in the new military government, which had seized power six months previously. He was old enough to have been her father, but she quickly became his mistress and they subsequently married. Eva promoted his cause and that of the new government on national radio. She formed an essential part of his bid to be president. In February 1946 Peron was elected and Eva became First Lady. She was just 26.

By now the poor girl from Los Toldos was dressed in the finest dresses and jewellery Argentina could provide. She also discovered an extraordinary capacity for addressing massive crowds. The poor heard her gladly. Organized labour, the poor workers, provided the foundation of Peronist political power. Critics called the supporters of the Perons *los descamisados*, 'the shirtless ones'. She gloried in the description.

By now she was *Evita* to the people, an affectionate diminutive. She went on a tour of Europe drawing huge crowds in Spain. She had an audience with Pope Pius XII, looking like a faithful daughter of the Church (which she probably believed herself to be in her own way). Many in the Catholic Church did love and idolize her. But she was a threat to the Church too. A young woman as 'spiritual leader of the nation'?

In July 1948 the Eva Peron Foundation was created, one of the most astonishing charitable institutions of the twentieth century. It provided money for anyone whom Eva thought deserved it. It built houses for poor families, schools, hospitals and homes for the aged. Its governance remained in the sole hands of its founder. By the time of Eva's death, the income of the foundation was equivalent to one third of the entire Argentine national budget. Nobody could avoid making a contribution if they wanted to trade successfully. Everyone had to praise the good works in which the First Lady was engaged. She allowed no dissent.

Eva worked from early morning to the early hours of the next morning, signing authorizations for a new house or medicines or hospital treatment or almost anything else. The poor had to present themselves to her personally. Many waited hours, even days, to meet her. She would hand out bank notes as additional gifts. It was a lottery as to who got help. Hardly any significant accounts were kept. There is no doubt it did some good. Wealth was redistributed but it was reckless and disorganized and harmed the overall Argentine economy.

By the time her husband was re-elected in 1952 Eva was dying from cancer of the womb. Within weeks of her death there were requests to the Vatican that she should be canonized immediately as a saint. The scale of the mourning for her surprised even her husband. He always looked a diminished figure afterwards.

In one of her final speeches before her death Eva said, 'I will come again and I will be millions'. It sounds messianic. It was. The millions were *los descamisados.*

Eva saw her legacy incarnated in the poor. She had done much to raise the political awareness of Argentinian women. They had got the vote, no matter how poor they were. Many of the 'Mothers of the Disappeared' who bravely marched outside the Presidential Palace under a later military dictatorship would not have revered Eva, but her engagement in politics and social action created a lasting determination among Argentinian women to be heard. Eva Peron was a flawed character, impulsive, headstrong and impatient with opposition. But her drive and ambition was shaped by injustice and social stigma. This poor, illegitimate girl changed her country.

Wealth, jewellery and fine clothes seemed to bore her in the end. In the final years of her life she dressed much more simply, as she dedicated herself to helping the poor. The way in which she lived was unsustainable, even without her cancer. The experience of poverty and social stigma never left Eva. Whatever her faults, she never forgot the poor from whom she came. That is why they blessed her.

> *God of the poor, take our flawed humanity*
> *and shape our best instincts so that we may be*
> *of service to those most in need. Amen.*

9

The Tenderness of God

U. A. Fanthorpe

Luke 14.7–14

My childhood years were spent in my native Cornwall. Like many other local people in Newquay in the 1950s, my parents offered bed and breakfast to holidaymakers who arrived by the thousand without accommodation. It was a useful way of supplementing income. But I recall little affection for these guests who helped to boost the local economy. Cornish attitudes towards holiday-makers were ambivalent. Sometimes they descended into resentment. You began to feel your town was not your own. All this was unsayable. Anyone who may have voiced such feelings would have found local people denying they thought like that at all.

The poet U. A. Fanthorpe captured this Cornish sentiment (I am sure it applies in other tourist desti-nations too) with accuracy in her poem 'Lostwithiel in February'. I was transported back to childhood when I read it. The writer is a tourist aimlessly going around the few Lostwithiel shops open in the winter, 'the unmonied half-life of the partitioned year'. The writer is conscious of the reticence of shopkeepers, pausing before they answer a question and aware of unheard, unspoken comments from passers-by. And the poem ends:

> … we can hear the authentic Cornish snarl,
> Razor's edge language of the occupied.

This poem, published in her collection *Safe As Houses* in 1995, is characteristic of the penetrating observation found in Fanthorpe's work. Such insight comes at a price for the poet. The keen-eyed often find themselves outsiders or cast to the margins. The two sensitive visitors to Lostwithiel (Fanthorpe and her companion) are uncomfortable in the poem while the natives feel invaded.

Ursula Askham Fanthorpe was born in 1929. Her father was a barrister and her mother a civil servant. Her unusual second name came from her mother's family, traceable back to Roger Askham, author of *The Schoolmaster* and a tutor to Queen Elizabeth I. Born in relatively comfortable circumstances, Ursula Fanthorpe (she preferred to be known to the public as U. A.) seemed to have had a predictable enough life mapped out for her following her graduation with a first class honours degree from St Anne's College, Oxford. A career as an English teacher at Cheltenham Ladies' College was steadily built. But eight years after becoming head of the English department she resigned, 'a middle-aged drop out' as she liked to describe herself.

She eventually found work, first as a receptionist and then as a clerk in a neurological hospital in Bristol. She recorded details of patients who fascinated her more than they knew. It was an ideal job for the sort of poet she became. Her first collection of poems, *Side Effects*, was published in 1978 when she was already in her 50th year. A decade later she devoted herself to poetry full-time, such was her success. She was nominated for the Professorship of Poetry at Oxford when James Fenton was elected. *The Guardian* campaigned for her to be Poet Laureate when Andrew Motion eventually succeeded Ted Hughes. So she had her share of modest fame. Yet some literary critics seemed to consider her too conventional, accessible and perhaps too English to be put in the first rank.

She had a long and loving partnership with Rosemarie Bailey (R. V. Bailey) whom she met at Cheltenham.

They registered their civil partnership in 2006. Society's recognition of their relationship came late.

Every Christmas, U. A. Fanthorpe and R. V. Bailey included a poem with their Christmas greetings to their friends. They are gifts to the Christmas preacher. Brevity is an art she mastered. These poems are grounded in the mystery of the incarnation and frequently take a figure from the margins of the action to the centre of the story. Fanthorpe was a Quaker, who believed the whole of life was sacramental. In 'Angels Song', Christ's birth prefigures his death. The angels, 'intimates of heaven', as she describes them with such attractive precision, are puzzled by the human fuss surrounding the birth of Jesus. They say:

> We sing a harder carol now;
> Holy the donkey in the hay;
> Holy the manger made of wood,
> Holy the nails, the blood, the clay.

This is taken even further in 'The Wicked Fairy at the Manger'. This fairy brings an unusual gift to the Christ child. It is the gift of identifying him with all that is disrespected, marginal, derided.

> No wife, kids, home;
> No money sense. Unemployable.

Friends, yes. But the wrong sort –
The workshy, women, wogs,
Petty infringers of the law ...
... his end?
I think we will make it
Public, prolonged, painful.

Right, said the baby. That was roughly
What we had in mind.

There is a lot of pain in Fanthorpe's poetry – and deep attention to people who suffer. A poem about Patience Strong begins with a searing indictment of her sentimental home spun verse: 'No doubt such rubbish sells. She must be feathering her inglenook'. But the setting moves to the outpatients department in a hospital where the poet brings a cup of tea to a working man in his 50s. He is an epileptic, and would have liked to serve as an ambulance driver. He realizes he would have been a handicap 'but I would have liked to help'. He takes out a precious booklet wrapped in cellophane and gently opens it. It contains Patience Strong poems and he says 'See, this is what keeps me going'. We, and the poet, are likewise ashamed of ourselves for our snobbery.

It is her tenderness towards common humanity which is one of U. A. Fanthorpe's most endearing qualities. She observes suffering people not with the cool detachment of a superior mind but through the prism of an incarnate Lord. Free from dogma as a Quaker, she never freed herself from Jesus Christ. U. A. Fanthorpe was for me a poet of the incarnation.

> *Tender God, reach out to those on the margins*
> *of society, especially the lost and the lonely.*
> *Enlarge our hearts and give us insight, for*
> *you were born as one of us out of love for this*
> *disordered world. Amen.*

10

Meanness and Mercy

Luke the Evangelist

Luke 19.1–10

It took me a while to work out that my faith had been shaped by Luke the gospel writer though I had not realized it. The process began during my training for ordination when I studied the New Testament seriously for the first time. Redaction criticism was then relatively new. We looked at the authors of the different gospels as creative writers rather than simply recorders of events with no editorial intent. Since Luke wrote almost one quarter of the New Testament (the Acts of the Apostles and his gospel are quite lengthy) he has had an enduring influence on the whole of the Christian Church. As a student reading the gospels in parallel, and able to compare one with another, I began to realize I often preferred Luke's accounts of the miracles or parables or of events in the ministry of Jesus. It took me a while to work out why.

At first I thought it was because Luke was self-consciously an historian. At the beginning of both his gospel and the Acts of the Apostles Luke presents his credentials. He is the only one of the gospel writers to say why he writes: it is to give an ordered account based on eyewitness testimony and his thorough investigations of 'the events that have taken place among us' (Luke 1.1).

I like an orderly narrative. Luke may not be writing history in a dispassionate, analytical way, but he is writing with a purpose since he wants those who read his work to believe that Jesus is the Christ, the promised one of God.

Luke's distinctive way of telling this story connects with me. I suppose I would not think I owed so much to him if I had not read the other gospels. He suits many contemporary Western people since he does not expect his readers to know Jewish traditions well. Matthew's gospel is very Jewish by comparison. Luke writes in more sophisticated Greek than Mark, the first of the gospel writers, whose message is stark and disturbing. Luke seems to inhabit a more sophisticated world. That is reflected in the dedication of his work to 'Theophilus, your Excellency'. He also seems very familiar with the world of money and wealth, even if he believes it is a dangerous one.

Without Luke, Christmas would be a very different festival: no stable; no manger; no shepherds; no heavenly host. Our liturgies would be very different too: no Magnificat, or Song of Mary; no Nunc Dimittis, Simeon's song in the temple when Jesus is presented as an eight-day-old baby. For that matter, there would be no Benedictus either, the Song of Zechariah, father of John the Baptist, filled with the Holy Spirit when he is given the power of speech again. Nor would we have the one precious story from the later childhood of Jesus when his parents take him to the Temple in Jerusalem and he goes missing in order to debate theology with the religious teachers.

Human tenderness in the company of divine revelation characterizes the way Luke tells his story. That's true in the major Lucan contribution to the resurrection appearances, namely the encounter with the risen Christ on the road to Emmaus. The disciples do not recognize the stranger until they break bread, and then he is gone. Luke does not criticize them for their lack of insight. He makes allowances for frail human beings encountering the mystery of the incarnation and resurrection.

Luke notices the little people who make the ministry of Jesus possible. Who was it who provided for

Jesus and his disciples as they went from place to place? Luke mentions that not only did Jesus travel from town to town with the Twelve but also with 'a number of women who had been set free from evil spirits and infirmities: Mary, known as Mary of Magdala ... Joanna, the wife of Chuza a steward of Herod's, Susanna, and many others' (Luke 8.2, 3). No other gospel writer mentions Joanna or Susanna. Nor do the others point out, as Luke does, that these women provided for Jesus and his disciples 'out of their own resources' (Luke 8.3).

Perhaps this human sensitivity in Luke means that it is not at all surprising that he, alone of the gospel writers, gives us the parable of the Good Samaritan as well as the parable of the Prodigal Son. Both are stories of human sin and foolishness met by astonishing generosity. Luke cannot bear meanness. His gospel is laced with encouragement to give charitably to others. Only in Luke do we get John the Baptist teaching his followers to share their goods with others: 'Whoever has two coats must share with him who has none, and whoever has food must do the same' (Luke 3.11).

The story of Zacchaeus, the rich superintendent of taxes, is found only in Luke. Zacchaeus is curious about Jesus and amazed when Jesus tells him that he will come to his house. The upshot is that Zacchaeus gives half his possessions away. If he has defrauded anyone he promises he will give them four times what he owes in return. He is told by Jesus, 'Salvation will come to this house today' (Luke 19.9).

It isn't simply the giving away of money which matters for Luke. The parable of the Pharisee and the Tax Collector is found only in Luke, and speaks of something more fundamental. The Pharisee fasted twice a week and was regular in his charitable giving but despised those who did not observe the letter of the law. The tax collector, extortioner though he was, working for a foreign power and creaming off profits for himself, simply pleads for God's mercy. He was the one who would be justified because he humbled himself. In Luke's world there is no point in charity if you are proud of it.

I fail miserably to lead the kind of Christian life which Luke commends with such clarity, humanity and sympathy. Even so, a Lucan discipleship is the sort to which I aspire. It rings true with a Saviour who gives his whole life away, and holds back nothing in his own self-giving. We do not really know who Luke was or whether to identify him with the 'Luke' mentioned sometimes in Paul's letters. It is plausible since the Acts of the Apostles suggests Luke may have been an eyewitness of some of the events he describes. The problem is that the picture of Paul we gain from his letters is rather different from the way in which Luke represents him in Acts. But how we see ourselves and how others see us can be very different.

It does not much matter that we know so little about Luke the gospel writer, where he was born and what he did with his life. We possess his gospel, written because he was so caught up in the story of Jesus Christ and his death and resurrection. It was a life-changing experience he wanted to share with as many other people as possible. Luke's gospel is as fresh and challenging now as when he first put pen to paper for his Excellency Theophilus.

> *Lord of the scriptures, we praise you for Luke*
> *the evangelist and all we learn of you through*
> *his writings; may we heed your warnings*
> *against meanness with money and meanness*
> *of spirit; enlarge our hearts and minds*
> *that with Zacchaeus we may imitate your*
> *amazing generosity. Amen.*

11

The Price of Generosity
Phyllis Simmons

Matthew 5.38–48

Phyllis finds her place in this book as a representative of the many unknown saints in the congregations of the Church of England (and other churches) throughout this country and in every generation. Already a widow, she must have been in her late 60s at the time of my ordination in 1975. She lived in the parish of Christ the Carpenter, Dogsthorpe, on the outskirts of Peterborough. The parish consisted of three separate council estates built in the 1950s, 1960s and 1970s. A daughter church to All Saints' Peterborough, it had been built in 1958 and became a separate parish in 1973. I arrived as the first curate of this new parish which by then had a population of around 15,000. Most of the work was provided by local engineering firms such as Perkins Engines. The church had a surprisingly large congregation, given its setting, but it had benefitted from a series of outstanding clergy.

Phyllis sang in the choir (though her singing voice was not one of her greatest assets), came to the Eucharist on at least one occasion during the week as well as both main services on Sunday and was consistently cheerful in outlook and demeanour. She didn't get involved much in the organizational life of the church. She gave her whole life to serving others.

Her home was modest and in truth not very comfortable, though she seemed to have little interest in material possessions. Her adult son was quite affluent; although he lived some distance away he did not neglect his mother at all. For years she didn't sleep in her own bed, but went to her neighbour's house, something she'd started doing after her neighbour was widowed. This prevented Phyllis from going away or staying much with her own son, since her neighbour didn't want to be left on her own. Phyllis put her neighbour's needs first, though her neighbour never seemed very grateful. But Phyllis never appeared to look for gratitude for her generosity, which was showered on a great many people.

Shortly before my ordination, my vicar asked the congregation to invite their new curate for Sunday lunch to their homes and other meals during the week since he was a helpless bachelor. It wasn't a parish of dinner parties but the congregation was astonishingly hospitable. At the Thursday evening Eucharist I would usually find a box of groceries left for me by Phyllis with a note telling me of people who were ill or who may need some pastoral help. She never put pressure on any of the clergy. Nor did she think it was the priest's job to visit and not hers. But she lived her life for others, engaged in practical help and rarely offered much advice. I doubt she knew many of Oscar Wilde's aphorisms, but she would instinctively have understood at least one of them: 'It is always a silly thing to give advice, but to give good advice is absolutely fatal'.

On one occasion I arrived at the home of a parishioner who was only a few days from her death from cancer. This lady was a daily communicant. Towards the end of her life I would sometimes sit with her. She was beyond conversation and could scarcely eat or drink. I would pray the evening collects from the Book of Common Prayer and she would either join in or open her eyes and smile at the familiar cadences of the collect for peace. 'Give unto thy servants that peace which the world cannot give' took on a new meaning when said with a faithful, dying Christian.

One evening on arrival her husband showed me into the kitchen. Phyllis had visited, having travelled on the bus from the other side of the estate. She had brought an apple pie and a jug of hot custard. Her husband was both amused and bemused. His wife was beyond apple pie and custard but Phyllis knew he liked it and had provided it in gargantuan quantity. The strangeness of this gift was offset by the greater gift of Phyllis' practical concern and the gift of her time. She did not linger. She did not intrude. She prayed for people and did whatever she could to help them. She was one of the reasons why that parish was so alive with fellowship and faith, for there were others like her there too, many of them.

Phyllis never seemed to have a bad word for anyone, nor to engage in gossip. Only once did I hear her pass comment. She was frustrated by a very devout and much younger woman who didn't seem to translate her many hours in church into the sort of practical Christianity Phyllis understood: 'She must be careful that she doesn't become so heavenly minded that she's no earthly use'.

My knowledge of Phyllis' history and wider life is very limited. She didn't speak about herself and wasn't very forthcoming when you asked her. If she could be criticized it would be on the grounds that she had not learned to receive very well. It was all giving. She was generous with money, time and effort beyond measure. She did not spare herself.

People were often astonished by Phyllis' generosity, even embarrassed by it. Her generosity did not make her particularly popular. Phyllis returned to my mind when I was reading Tom Wright's book *Jesus and the Victory of God*. There he speaks of a key characteristic which Jesus expected in his disciples: astonishing generosity.

There is something almost perverse in what we read in the Sermon on the Mount: 'If anyone strikes you on the right cheek, turn the other also; and if anyone wants to sue you and take your coat, give your cloak as well; and if anyone forces you to go one mile, go also the second mile' (Matthew 5.39, 40). Tom Wright says that even when people use us or take advantage of us, they 'must be met with astonishing generosity'.

It isn't exceptional kindness which reflects the generosity of God in his people. It is the willingness to be of service to others when it is utterly unrewarding. This is the pattern of the Passion and death of Jesus Christ. Few of his disciples are called to imitate him to the point of death, though martyrs are many.

But, in the example of Phyllis Simmons and many others, I have seen vivid reflections of the generosity of God himself and the change it can make to the world. It catches people's attention, stops them in their tracks, and can cause resentment and consternation as well as wonder and joy. Phyllis taught me as a young curate that God's astonishing generosity in Jesus Christ is not always received with joy by human beings. Perhaps that's why generosity and the way of the Cross go together.

> *Generous God, you gave us Jesus Christ yet*
> *he was rejected; prevent us being discouraged*
> *when we show generosity to others and meet*
> *hostility, and sustain us when we discover*
> *the way of giving is also the way of the Cross.*
> *Amen.*

12

Patience and Grace

James Paget

Romans 8.24–30

James Paget is known as the father of modern pathology. His name is also remembered because rather unpleasant diseases of the bone and breast are named after him. There's even such a thing as Paget's abscess. Quite how he may have felt about this use of his name is uncertain, but it's a sign of his leadership in medical research and surgical innovation.

James Paget was born in 1814 in Great Yarmouth. He was the son of a brewer and ship owner in the town. At the age of 16 he was apprenticed to a general practitioner. Medicine seems to have absorbed his mind from an early age, as did his loyalty to the Christian faith. Whether his chosen profession was a response to the command of Jesus to his disciples to heal the sick is not recorded. But he saw himself doing a work for his Lord in ensuring that the well-being of the body was regarded with the same importance as the well-being of mind and spirit.

At the age of 20, Paget gained entry as a student to St Bartholomew's Hospital in London. Apprentice doctors and surgeons in hospitals were then left fairly much to themselves to observe their seniors, to learn by practising on patients (a rather horri-fying thought) and to do whatever study they wished. There were medical prizes for new discov-eries but scarcely any formal teaching or training programme. Paget excelled through his combi-nation of self-discipline and imagination. Perhaps it was the inadequacy of his own medical training which caused him later to become such a brilliant teacher and tutor to other medical students. He knew how to encourage and supervise. He was a man of sophistication in an age when not all surgeons were thought to be sophisticated. He loved music, literature and theology. He had a wide hinterland. He used the new invention of the time, the modern microscope, to develop the disciplines of pathology.

James Paget began his medical career before the days of anaesthetics. It wasn't until 1846 that the very first ether anaesthetics were administered in Scotland

and London. It took decades for anaesthetics to cease to be seriously dangerous in themselves. It meant that at the beginning of Paget's professional life very few surgical operations were feasible. A growth on the surface of the skin, the amputation of a limb or cutting into the body quickly to remove bladder stones were about the only possibilities. No one thought it feasible to operate on the abdomen or the chest. In any case, surgeons had to be exceptionally quick with their knives since most patients were strapped down. Many died on the operating table or soon afterwards. The screams must have been agonizing. An effective surgeon had to be calm and quick while the patient yelled in agony. It was Paget who suggested that removing the tumour rather than the limb would be rather more effective. Local anaesthetics made his suggestions feasible. He believed in precision, and pathologists acknowledge that some of his original work has even now been hardly superseded.

James Paget was a friend of both Charles Darwin and Thomas Huxley. Huxley was the greater controversialist of the two. He engaged in the famous public debate about evolution with Samuel Wilberforce, the Bishop of Oxford. Wilberforce unwisely asked Huxley whether he thought he was descended from an ape on his father's or his mother's side. As it turned out Sir James Paget's son, Francis, became Bishop of Oxford a few decades later. Another son, Luke, became Bishop of Chester. It was a devout family.

James Paget could never understand the so-called conflict between religion and science. He emphasized that there was nothing in science to make anyone adverse to faith. He explained to young men training for ordination that their battle would never be with science or scientists but with the mistaken inferences derived from scientific knowledge which got used as arguments against religion. Paget anticipated Richard Dawkins by more than a century. He would have thought Dawkins was making a simple category mistake, confusing one sort of knowledge for another.

Paget became so eminent that he was consulted on all sorts of controversial issues. A Norfolk rector, The Revd Arthur Loftus, from Fincham, was accused of keeping two women who were prostitutes as servants in his rectory. Mr Loftus brought his local doctor to defend him in the consistory court. Because the rector's wife had denied him conjugal rights for three years, his doctor had prescribed the occasional employment of a decent woman to release the much frustrated rector's natural affections. Apparently this was prescribed by doctors rather more frequently in early Victorian England than we may imagine. James Paget pronounced on the subject and said:

> I would just as soon prescribe theft or lying,
> or anything else that God has forbidden.
> If men will practise unfaithfulness or
> uncleanness it must be of their own choice
> and their sole responsibility ... chastity does
> no harm to mind or body ...

Mr Loftus was deprived of his rectory, stipend and any further preferment. Fincham has never seen such excitement since.

James Paget did not believe that moral and spiritual health were guaranteed by physical well-being. However, he did recognize that they were interconnected, and that people themselves had responsibility for their own healing. He understood that while surgery often needed to be quick, true healing took time. Those he treated were not called patients accidentally. Patience was needed.

If there was one virtue which characterized James Paget it was patience. He was patient in his obser-vation and research. He was patient with his students. He was patient with his family. His father fell into serious debt just when James's career was beginning to take off. James Paget kept himself poor for 14 years while he paid off his father's debts. He knew how to wait for better times. He understood the value of patience.

James Paget's career developed slowly. Only later in life did his reputation go into overdrive. National and international honours came his way but his character didn't alter. He would still give time to people. He understood that God is patient with his people, because he loves us. Love requires patience, as does healing. Those closest to us often suffer our irritability but, faced by serious and long-lasting problems, many of us are most patient with those we love the best. Patience and love are more closely linked than we sometimes seem to realize.

Eighty years after his death Sir James Paget was remembered in the area in which he grew up when the local hospital at Gorleston was named after him. I doubt he would be troubled by such delay. He was never a man in a rush. Nor was Jesus, who took 30 years before he began his public ministry. It was the gift of Paget's time and his patient observation which led to the discipline of modern pathology. His spiritual understanding of the human condition and what God had done for us in Jesus Christ was the source of his patience with people. In the miracle of the human body he saw the glory of God. As St Irenaeus expressed it, 'the glory of God is a human being fully alive'. The legacy of James Paget is not simply medical.

Christ our healer, give us wholeness in body, mind and spirit; instil in us such patience that we may grow in your likeness and do your will. Amen.

13

Living from Others
Charles Williams

1 Corinthians 12.12–26

Some writers and artists are destined never to be very famous themselves but to exercise great influence on those who do achieve celebrity status. W. H. Auden, C. S. Lewis and J. R. R. Tolkien all acknowledged a debt to Charles Williams. Williams died in 1945 and left a huge literary legacy. He wrote fiction, theology, biographies, plays and poetry. The Charles Williams Society maintains devotion to him. He is fascinating enough for a series of academic articles and books to have been written about him in recent years. But in comparison with the success of the *Narnia* stories of C. S. Lewis or *The Lord of the Rings* trilogy by Tolkien there has been no commercial interest in Williams' novels. They are allegorical fantasies in which the inter-section of the supernatural and natural orders is taken as read. They are set within the contemporary world. Perhaps that latter aspect is their undoing, though they also need unpacking as they are not appealingly written for the present generation. It is Williams' theological writing which stands the test of time better.

I don't know why I first read *The Descent of the Dove*, Charles Williams' short history of the Holy Spirit in the Church, but I did so while I was training for ordination. It wasn't on any reading list. I knew nothing about its author at the time. I think I picked up a second-hand copy in Blackwell's in Oxford for a paltry sum.

I found it both a bewildering and exciting read. It was bewildering since I didn't know enough Church history to understand the nuances. Williams assumes quite a lot of historical and literary knowledge in his readers, perhaps an intriguing tribute to the cultural depth of English Christianity in the 1930s. Yet there was something personally embracing in his way of setting out the history of the Christian Church. I felt included in the story. It seemed that Williams thought he was telling me about members of my family. I had not read a history of the Church before which acknowledged its shortcomings and failures but also recognized the Holy Spirit guiding and shaping the life of the faithful at one and the same time. I felt drawn to Williams' theory of 'co-inherence', even if I didn't really understand it for he never defined it clearly enough for my late-twentieth-century sceptical mind. Even so, I knew somehow the whole book was the definition. That I was a late-twentieth-century Christian who was connected and related to all those who had believed in Christ and were still a present reality in the communion of saints was precisely what Williams was setting out to demonstrate. I knew it was a book I would read again.

It was only much later that I discovered that W. H. Auden claimed to read *The Descent of the Dove* every year. Auden had met Charles Williams for the first time when he had been asked by the Oxford University Press to prepare *The Oxford Book of Light Verse*. Auden was captivated by Williams and wrote, 'for the first time in my life ... I felt I was in the presence of personal sanctity ... I had met many good people who had made me feel ashamed of my own shortcomings, but in the presence of this man – we never discussed anything but literary business – I did not feel ashamed. I felt transformed into a person who was incapable of doing anything base or unloving'. Others felt the same about Williams, notably T. S. Eliot and C. S. Lewis, neither of whom had much regard for the other.

This man with such an impact on the lives of others had a modest background himself. Born in 1886, he was educated at St Albans School and went on to University College, London. There was very little money in his family which meant he couldn't complete his degree. Hence he was largely self-educated. He joined the Oxford University Press in his early 20s, initially as a proofreader, but his abilities were recognized and he became a literary editor of great renown. He worked for the Oxford University Press until his death in 1945. Williams married while he was still young and had a son, Michael, but his marriage to Florence Conway wasn't especially happy. That may have spurred his creativity even more keenly and made him live for his friends more devotedly.

It was Charles Williams who once said, 'It is regarded as Christian to live *for* others; it is not so often regarded as Christian doctrine that we live *from* others'. Living from others is much more difficult than living for them. Generally we don't mind living from those whom we love and admire. But it is much more difficult to receive from those we don't like, to listen to those with whom we may not agree, to keep company with those who offend us. But they also make us the people we are. If the Pauline imagery of the body of Christ has any meaning, then we know this to be true. We are members one of another within the baptized community of believers, but we are also deeply interconnected with every other human being made in the image and likeness of God. Charles Williams used to say, 'It's good when people say I will pray *for* you. It's best when they say I will pray *in* you'.

Such sayings expressed Williams' deep conviction about co-inherence, a term he used in a number of different and yet related ways. A child co-inheres within its mother for nine months before birth. Williams noted that no human creature has failed to spring from anything other than such a process of interior and totally interdependent growth. He used co-inherence to speak of the divine and human natures of Jesus Christ and the relationship between the persons of the Holy Trinity. Most of all, though, the idea is best expressed in the way in which the Christian believer is incorporated by baptism into Christ and dwells in Christ as Christ dwells in him or her. There is nothing solitary about the Christian experience. To live in love is to live in God, which means living both from others and praying in them. This is more than friendship. It is more than goodness. It is more than holiness. It is the life of the communion of saints anticipated within the world as it is.

> *Lord Jesus Christ, you call into friendship*
> *with you those whom we would never choose;*
> *help us learn and receive from those for whom*
> *we have no natural liking yet with whom we*
> *co-inhere as members of one body, your holy*
> *catholic and apostolic church. Amen.*

14

Courtesy and Character

Robin Ferrers

Colossians 4.5, 6

It is the custom in the House of Lords for the Lord Speaker to announce the death of a Member immediately after Prayers, at the beginning of the day's proceedings. The average age of peers means it's not an unusual event. Sometimes there is a murmur of sadness. A very loud collective sigh was heard from all corners of the House on 13 November 2012 when the death of Robert Washington Shirley, the 13th Earl Ferrers, was announced. He was Robin to all who knew him. He was held in deep affection. Just three weeks earlier he had paid his last visit to Parliament. In his wheelchair he was surrounded by colleagues queuing to speak to him. Robin was in his element. The word 'gregarious' might have been invented for him.

I only knew Robin in the last 13 years of his life, by which time he was already an institution. He was the

High Steward of Norwich Cathedral, a place he loved with every fibre of his being. He was a deeply loyal man – to his country, his Church, his wife and to all the places and people who had nurtured him. No bishop could have had a stronger or more sympathetic supporter. But perhaps above all it was his courtesy which impressed me (and many others) most. He treated people with immense respect and care.

Robin served in every Conservative adminis-tration – under five prime ministers – from Harold Macmillan to John Major. He always affected surprise that he had been given such responsibilities at all. But his capacity as a minister of state to steer unwelcome legislation through the House of Lords was enormous because he did so with such charm and humour. He loved his six years as a Minister in the Home Office even though he had to answer questions on the full range of that huge depart-ment's responsibilities. There were elephant traps everywhere. During questions he was once asked whether someone who spat at you in the street and hit you was guilty of an assault. Robin had no idea. Instead of offering a tortuous reply he rendered an extraordinary ditty his mother had taught him:

Julius Caesar
Let a Greaser

Right across the street
And hit Agrippa
On the Nipper
And knocked him off his seat.

Such an unexpected ministerial response not only created mirth but took the heat out of whatever was the problem of the day. Robin never considered himself quick-witted but he could be masterly. On another occasion there was a fuss about a large meteorite apparently coming towards Earth. How much notification would Parliament receive if it hit the country, he was asked. Robin said he was pretty certain Black Rod would have time to say 'Cheerio chaps'.

Robin was imposing in stature and came from a family, the Shirleys, whom he liked to say welcomed William the Conqueror to England. He came top of the poll when hereditary Conservative peers had to elect their quota following the reforms of Tony Blair's first government. He was loved but he never possessed the bucketloads of inner self-confidence some imagined. He understood that human beings have weaknesses. He knew his own and was aware of both the fragility and beauty of human life. Within his own family two of his daughters predeceased him. It caused him deep agony. This awareness of both fragility and beauty in the human condition was why the Christian faith made such sense to him. He loved glorious worship reflecting the grandeur and majesty of God. But he knew his need of redemption and forgiveness. His God was one who reaches out to fallen and sinful human beings and raises them up.

Robin could never understand a world in which commitments were transient or loyalty shallow. His time as a pupil at Winchester College shaped his life and character. Its founder, William of Wykeham, Winchester's bishop at the end of the fourteenth century, had a motto 'Manners makyth man'. In its day it was a revolutionary thought. It suggested that it wasn't noble birth, money, land or property which defined someone's worth. It was how they behaved towards others. Manners were found in a person's habitual behaviour and conduct reflecting their moral and spiritual character. An inwardly mean and spiteful human being would never sustain outward kindness and consideration towards others for long. The teaching of Jesus includes what became known as the Golden Rule – 'Always treat others as you would like them to treat you'. Robin lived by that. Manners makyth man. Manners made Robin.

After Robin died, Martin Narey, then Director General of the Prison Service, wrote about his experience as Robin's Private Secretary at the Home Office. He said:

> Robin was, by some measure, the most courteous man I ever met and one of the kindest. Officials in the Home Office loved him. For his part he insisted that anyone who worked into the evening offering him advice from the Officials Box later had to be entertained to a drink in his office. I worked for him for eighteen months. During all that time I never once saw him compromise his beliefs. He simply never said or did anything which he didn't think was the right thing to do. He was a great man.

One of the less well known of Robin's public offices was that of Grand Prior of England and Wales for the Order of St Lazarus of Jerusalem. The cross of the order has eight points. They exhort the wearer to exercise those virtues which are derived from the Sermon on the Mount.

- Contempt for riches of this world
- Gentleness of spirit
- Christian sympathy and compassion
- Ardent zeal for justice
- Mercy and pity

- Purity of heart
- Peace of mind
- The bearing of persecution for righteousness sake

Robin held to the Cross of Christ throughout his life. Jesus Christ transformed despair into hope. A Cross-shaped faith isn't a gloomy one, luxuriating in suffering and glorifying pain. The Cross is the symbol of liberation into God's kingdom, often pictured as a heavenly banquet. Given Robin's capacity as a party animal, it is not hard to picture him fizzing with even more life in the world to come.

> *Eternal God, through Jesus you invite us into your kingdom; may our lives be filled with the fine food of your word and sacraments and the heady delight of the good wine of your grace in anticipation of your heavenly banquet, where all are united in your love. Amen.*

15

The Indwelling Spirit
Charles Wesley

Acts 2.1–13

Charles Wesley's influence in my life, as on the lives of millions of other Christians, has come through his hymns. Only recently did I discover that, though he wrote somewhere between 6,000 and 9,000 hymns and sacred poems, he refused to publish his journals and letters in his lifetime and even instructed his family not to publish his journals after his death. While his elder brother, John, enjoyed the spotlight, Charles seemed to shun it. The consequences of their respective conversions in 1738 (Charles's took place three days before his elder brother's) contrasted more than initial appearance might suggest. While both experienced a quickening of faith prompting them (following the practice of George Whitefield) to preach in the open air on an itinerant basis, Charles possessed both a more emotionally volatile personality than his brother and a more modest and retiring spirit too. He also experienced a happy marriage, something denied to John Wesley. His family stability was one of the reasons why in the latter half of his life Charles was happy to stay at home.

When Charles was born in Epworth Rectory just before Christmas 1707, he was the 18th child of Samuel and Susanna Wesley. It looked at first as if he would not survive. Infant mortality was well known at Epworth. Only ten of Samuel and Susanna's children survived into adult life. Charles proved more robust than he looked, though he enjoyed ill-health throughout his life. Like many a creaking gate, he lived a long time.

Susanna was in charge of the children's education at Epworth. It was grounded in learning the scriptures. Charles's later education came at Westminster School and then Christ Church, Oxford. His personality was winning. In his attempts to live a more disciplined religious life, he gathered others around him. They quickly became known as the 'Holy Club' in Oxford. On John's return to his fellowship at Lincoln College after a spell as his father's curate, the elder brother assumed leadership of the Holy Club. Charles was content for John to do so.

The nature of their relationship seems to account for Charles accompanying John on the ill-fated mission to Georgia, where James Oglethorpe, the first governor of the British colony, invited them to come as missionaries and ministers of the gospel. Charles hoped to remain in Oxford but he wrote, 'my brother, who always had the ascendant over me, persuaded me to accompany him and Mr Oglethorpe to Georgia. I exceedingly dreaded entering into holy orders, but he overruled me here also, and I was ordained deacon by the Bishop of Oxford, Dr Potter, and the next Sunday, priest by the Bishop of London, Dr Gibson'.

The Georgian adventure was not a happy one for either John or Charles. Their ministries were not well received. In John's case a huge row over his alleged breach of promise by not marrying a woman called Sophy Hopkey added to his ignominy. The whole adventure was misconceived. Charles discovered he was little suited to the loneliness and hardships of missionary endeavour in hostile environments. James Oglethorpe recognized as much since he recommended that Charles get married since he was of such a social temper that the help of a good wife would mean a happier life in Christian service.

As it turned out, Charles would not marry until April 1749, following well over a decade of constant itinerant preaching. He then settled first in Bristol and later in London from 1771. Charles did not always see eye to eye with John over the way Methodism developed. He clashed with some of the more volatile of Methodism's lay leadership, well illustrated by a crisis in Norwich in 1760. Methodist lay preachers in the Norwich circuit had been administering the sacrament of Holy Communion without any authority to do so other than their own. John did not immediately arouse himself to action but a campaign led by Charles eventually prevented the practice. It was just one sign that Methodism would eventually become a separate ecclesial body.

As we sing Charles Wesley's hymns, we may be unaware of his capacity for biting satire. He vigorously opposed his brother John's illegal ordinations of Thomas Coke and others for the American Church towards the end of his life. The bitterness in Charles is evident.

> So easily are Bishops made
>> By men's or women's whim?
> Wesley his hands on Coke hath laid,
>> But who laid hands on him?

Hands on himself he laid, and took
    An Apostolic Chair:
And then ordained his creature Coke
    His Heir and Successor.

Such satirical compositions reveal his ecclesiology vividly, as do his hymns. Following his conversion in 1738 he was convinced that the Holy Spirit dwelt in the soul of the believer and brought the process of sanctification to fulfilment. His satire shows this did not mean a disregard for good order in the Church.

One of Charles's best loved hymns, 'And Can It Be?', dates from the time of his conversion. It was sung at my first celebration of the Eucharist as well as my enthronement in Norwich Cathedral, an acknowledgement of my family's Methodist roots. 'And Can It Be?' speaks of the freedom the believer finds in Christ. It is personal. Christ finds 'me'. But the universal character of our salvation in Him is never neglected.

And can it be, that I should gain
    An interest in the Saviour's blood?
Died He for me? – Who caused His pain!
    For me? – Who Him to death pursued.
Amazing love! How can it be

That Thou, my God, should'st die for
me?

The mystery of salvation is beyond our capacity to understand. 'Who can explore his strange design?' is the question in the second verse. Then Wesley emphasizes the lavish and undeserved grace of Christ – 'so free, so infinite his grace'. There is a kenotic quality to his Christology. He says that Christ 'emptied himself of all but love'.

Despite his religious upbringing, his ordination and commitment to the Christian life, Charles Wesley had still felt bound in spirit. The experience of his quickening of faith at his conversion was like being released from prison. He uses the image to powerful effect.

Long my imprison'd spirit lay,
Fast bound in sin and nature's night:
Thine eye diffused a quickening ray;
I woke; the dungeon flamed with light;
My chains fell off, my heart was free,
I rose, went forth, and follow'd Thee.

The final verse speaks of the liberation of the believer, who does not trust in his own righteousness for salvation but solely in what Christ has done for him:

No condemnation now I dread,
Jesus, and all in Him, is mine:
Alive in Him, my Living Head,
And clothed in righteousness Divine,
Bold I approach th'eternal throne,
And claim the crown, through Christ, my
  own.

Another hymn by Charles, 'O thou who camest from above', was sung at the concluding Eucharist each year at my theological college, Cuddesdon (just outside Oxford), when the stoles made for our subsequent ordinations were brought forward and laid on the altar. In asking Jesus to 'confirm my heart's desire to work, and speak, and think for thee', Charles Wesley did not restrict the plea to the ordained clergy. But, as we have seen, he did have a very high doctrine of episcopal ordination. So the hymn fits. Its reference to 'an inextinguishable blaze' finds its origin in Leviticus 6.13 where the Lord tells Moses 'a perpetual fire shall be kept burning on the altar: it shall not go out'. For Wesley, the altar where the flame needed to be kept burning was the altar of the heart, kindled with fire as a result of the coming of the Holy Spirit at Pentecost and experienced afresh in each believer's conversion.

O Thou who camest from above

The fire celestial to impart,
kindle a flame of sacred love
on the mean altar of my heart.

There let it for thy glory burn
with inextinguishable blaze,
and trembling to its source return
in humble prayer and fervent praise.

Towards the end of his life, Charles Wesley defined religion as 'happiness in God, or in the knowledge or love of God. It is faith working by love; producing righteousness, peace and joy in the Holy Ghost'. Through the legacy of his hymns Charles Wesley still speaks from soul to soul.

Holy Spirit, kindle the fire in our hearts so that our love for you may flow outwards in service and inwards in conviction so that we work and speak and think in our Saviour Jesus Christ. Amen.

16

God Looking on Us

Douglas Feaver

Luke 22.54–62

Douglas Feaver became Bishop of Peterborough in 1972. It was the year I went to Cuddesdon Theological College as a Peterborough-sponsored ordinand at the age of 21. I never met my diocesan bishop until the first day of my ordination retreat three years later. The retreat was held at the Palace in Peterborough itself. But my bishop had a surprising insight into my theological training. Those were the days when Michael Ramsey, as Archbishop of Canterbury, took all the bishops to Cuddesdon for a residential meeting. It was part of his rather romantic connection with the place. Douglas Feaver stayed in my room, read some of my essays which he found in folders on the shelves and left comments upon them. He liked the historical essays but thought I was being infected with liberal theology.

Douglas Feaver had a reputation for being the rudest

bishop in the Church of England. He didn't usually shake hands, except with the Queen. He could get through a confirmation service (always from the Book of Common Prayer without communion) in 35 minutes and didn't linger long at the bunfight afterwards. He had a visceral antipathy to liturgical revision and was conservative in almost every way. He was reputedly the last bishop to argue for capital punishment from the Bishops' bench in the House of Lords.

He was loved by many of his clergy, and took his role as *Pastor Pastorum* seriously. He was capable of being immensely kind, but was also very shy. This probably explained his abruptness and occasionally inappropriate humour. Many lay people found him unfathomable. But my ordination retreats introduced me to what living an ordered Prayer Book spirituality felt like.

Thomas Cranmer expected morning prayer and evening prayer to be public services offered every day in every parish church. The conflation of the monastic offices into these two public services with the whole of the Psalter recited every month was part of his vision for every parish church to be a religious community in itself. The monasteries may have been dissolved but Cranmer wanted to see villages and town churches alike becoming places of daily worship and praise. He expected lay congregations to attend twice a day. That's what should mark a Prayer Book parish church as truly distinctive.

Born as the First World War began, Douglas Feaver grew up in Bristol and attended St Mary Redcliffe where he learned the Christian faith. He took Firsts in modern history and theology at Oxford and was ordained to be the curate of St Alban's Abbey, continuing there as sub dean before becoming the Vicar of St Mary's, Nottingham. It was from Nottingham that he moved to Peterborough as its bishop.

Some people are loyal to the Book of Common Prayer out of devotion to the beauty of its language or because they cherish an unchanging tradition. Douglas Feaver was often considered reactionary but you only had to live with him for a few days to understand that the Book of Common Prayer was the foundation of his prayer life, worship, spirituality and discipleship. He didn't just say the collects. He prayed them and pondered their words. He prayed the Psalms. His sermons were generally based upon the collects or the Psalms. They possessed scarcely any reference to contemporary events. There was a timelessness to his teaching: 'Treasure there is beyond dreams concentrated in the collects: with more than enough sustenance for the soul as long as this life lasts. Learning by heart the collect for the day is more than an optional pious exercise; it is an essential discipline for all who would thoroughly learn Christ and grow in his grace'.

A booklet of his devotional reflections upon all the collects of the Book of Common Prayer was published a few years after his death. A good example of his theological and homiletic style is found in his reflection on the collect for the Third Sunday in Lent: 'We beseech thee, Almighty God, look upon the hearty desires of thy humble servants, and stretch forth the right hand of thy Majesty, to be our defence against all our enemies; through Jesus Christ our Lord. Amen'.

In his brief exposition, Douglas Feaver draws attention to what he considered a surprising word, 'look'. He goes on to reveal some of his own keen convictions (or prejudices, as some may describe them) before helping us to recognize the self-centredness of so many of our prayers.

> We would expect to pray, 'Listen to the
> hearty desires of thy humble servants'.
> But the verb is 'look'. We are so careful to

compose public prayers telling the Lord
exactly what we want him to do, with an
eye to those who overhear us, so that they
might be impressed by our social concern
with advertised issues. Too often we do
not know what to ask: and to this our so
called 'intercessions' bear witness. Put into
Judaea in our Lord's day, we would pray,
instructing God what to do with the priests
and Pharisees, to insert a backbone into
Pilate; to stop storms, to abolish pain and
death; and to join with Simon Peter in his
'this be far from Thee, Lord'.

Because the prayer asks God to look upon us rather
than listen to us, God can take the initiative to
stretch forth his right hand in majesty. Our weakness
is rewarded by God's strength. Thus Simon Peter
ceases to sink in the water. Christ looks upon his
mother and the disciple whom he loved from the
Cross and they then see each other in a new light as
he sees them. Like the penitent thief, it is to Christ
who was crucified that we look for help, and not
to those who stand around. That's why Douglas
Feaver argues from this collect that Christ is the
defence against all our enemies, though the most
difficult enemy is likely to emerge from the corner
we least expect. Such was Simon Peter's experience

in the palace of the High Priest when the servant
girl's accusation led to his denial of Christ. Douglas
Feaver concluded his reflection on this collect as
follows: 'Christ's cry of victory is "arise from the
dead": For dead we are; but in God's mercy we are
dead with Christ so that eternity is His and ours. He
is all in all. Upon him speechless upon the Cross the
Father looked. Christ in his crucifixion is the hearty
desire of the faithful servant, humble and despised,
and rejected of men, but received by God'.

Douglas Feaver's prose style was shaped by the Book
of Common Prayer and the Authorised Version of
the Bible. It belongs to another century, not even
the twentieth but one rather earlier. However,
when the listener tuned in to his wavelength she
heard a poetic preacher for whom words conveyed
the mystery of the Word of God. It was not hard
to see why he found the collects of the Alternative
Service Book so prosaic. The mystery and majesty
of God for Douglas Feaver was found in the mercy
we receive in Jesus Christ, a mercy both great and
undeserved.

> *God of majesty and glory, you meet us in your*
> *Son Jesus Christ; look upon us with mercy*
> *and help us to treasure the mystery of your*
> *undeserved and saving love. Amen.*

17

The Woman at the Well
Elsie Chamberlain

John 4.7–15

The Revd Elsie Chamberlain was the nearest thing to royalty the Congregational Union of England and Wales possessed in the 1950s and 1960s. She came to our manse in Cornwall when I was about six or seven years old. She was then President of the Congregational Union, the equivalent of the Archbishop of Canterbury, except that Congregationalists are opposed to such hierarchies. She preached twice in our church that Sunday. It was a huge occasion.

My parents were nervous about entertaining this luminary of the denomination who was a well-known voice on the BBC. Elsie worked in the Religious Broadcasting Department and was responsible for 'Lift Up Your Hearts', the forerunner of 'Thought for the Day'.

Elsie Chamberlain was born in 1910 in Islington. Her father was a post office clerk who belonged to the Church of England and attended his parish church, while her mother was a Congregationalist. After leaving school, Elsie became a dress designer. But her sense of vocation to Christian ministry was overwhelming. It was to Congregationalism she looked for its fulfilment. She had hardly any choice, since no other mainstream church at the time ordained women to a full ministry of word and sacrament.

The Congregational Union of England and Wales had agreed in 1913 to open its ministry to men and women alike, though it wasn't until 1917 that the first female Congregationalist minister, Constance Shacklock, was ordained.

Elsie Chamberlain studied theology at King's College, London, where many young men were also preparing for ordination in the Church of England. At least one of them made a friend of her, the rather exotically named John Leslie St Clair Garrington. They were eventually married in 1947. The Bishop of London, William Wand, was far from convinced that Garrington should be presented to a living while Elsie was a serving Congregational minister. She had begun her ministry in Liverpool in 1939, moving to be the minister at Friern Barnet in 1941.

While at King's she had become a friend of Margaret, Viscountess Stansgate, Tony Benn's formidable mother, whose husband was the Secretary of State for Air. This partly explains how Elsie became the very first female chaplain in the Royal Air Force, and the first anywhere in the armed services. The Archbishop of Canterbury, Geoffrey Fisher, demanded of the Air Minister that no communicant in the Church of England should be expected to attend communion services at which Elsie would preside. John Garrington was eventually appointed at All Saints, Hampton, thanks to a private patron. Elsie played her part as the vicar's wife while also working part-time as the minister of the Vineyard Congregational Church in Richmond. John and Elsie proved their marriage and ministerial partnership could work. He was appointed as Rector of Greensted in 1963. Elsie was always convinced that their marriage prevented her husband's further preferment.

Her appointment to the BBC's Religious Broadcasting Department in 1950 brought her to national prominence. She was the first woman to lead the BBC Daily Service. In the 1950s few people had experience of women leading worship at all. She did so, as she preached, without gimmicks or affectation and with directness. She built up a substantial following, working easily with others from different church traditions and denominations.

It was while she was still at the BBC that Elsie became the first ever woman to be the President of the Congregational Union and, it is sometimes claimed, the first ever female leader of a mainstream Christian denomination anywhere in the world. Congregationalism is grounded in independence. It believes the local church has all the marks of the church catholic as a self-governing body of believers. Perhaps only a deep vocation to ministry and a strong conviction of independence could have sustained the sort of ministry Elsie exercised. She met opposition from those who did not know her or thought her calling inappropriate but rarely from those to whom she ministered.

She left the BBC in 1967 at the time of the transformation of the Home Service into Radio 4. The series of separate programmes which had formed much of the morning output was gradually changing into the *Today Programme* with its focus on news and current affairs. Elsie disliked the change from advocacy of the Christian faith in 'Lift

Up Your Hearts' to the analysis of news in the light of faith in 'Thought for the Day'. She could not be part of it.

Nor was she willing to be part of the United Reformed Church, created in 1972 and perhaps the most significant product of a negotiated path to Christian unity. Elsie (like Viscountess Stansgate) cherished the rugged independence of Congregationalism. She joined the Congregational Federation, which consisted of around 300 churches who refused to join the new denomination. After her husband died she continued to minister to small churches, later living near the centre of Congregational Federation activities in Nottingham. She died in 1991.

Elsie worked for unity but understood the value of honest diversity. It is a gospel theme, well reflected in the surprising encounter Jesus has with a Samaritan woman at Jacob's well (John 4). Such free and uninhibited conversation between a Jewish male and a Samaritan woman was well outside any social or religious norm.

Jesus breaks a social and religious taboo by asking the Samaritan woman for a drink. A Jew would avoid a drinking vessel used by a Samaritan since that would make it ritually unclean. Jesus was never keen on such distinctions. He speaks of streams of living water leading to eternal life.

The Samaritan woman is very careful in what she says. She also seems keen not to lead this Jewish male into doing something he may regret. Jesus does not regard every distinction between Jews and Samaritans as of no account. But he shows how every human being is cherished and loved by God and that the possibility of salvation is open to everyone. His key move is to ask for a drink, first receiving hospitality rather than offering it.

Elsie Chamberlain didn't think the distinctions between the Churches didn't matter. If she had, she would have joined the United Reformed Church. She received hospitality from all the Churches when she could. She asked for many metaphorical drinks. For Elsie, the Church of Jesus Christ primarily consisted of believers in his saving power gathering together praising him, invoking him and witnessing to him. She believed the hospitality of God was greater than we can ever conceive or imagine.

> *Lord, you have created a diverse world yet*
> *draw us into union with each other and with*
> *you; we honour the calling of the first women*

to minister your word and sacrament, and
praise you for their courage and conviction.
Amen.

18

Friendship in Christ
Launcelot Fleming

John 15.12–17

When I began my ministry in Norwich in January 2000 I expected people to mention my immediate predecessors, though I was taken by surprise when Launcelot Fleming's name was recalled so often. He had left Norwich in 1970 to become Dean of Windsor after 11 years in the diocese. (That was one of the shorter ministries of Bishops of Norwich in modern times. There have only been 12 Bishops of Norwich, including me, since 1792.) Thirty years after his departure, Launcelot Fleming's memory remained fresh. Gradually I came to realize hardly anyone spoke of his sermons or his teaching. Apart from the establishment of group and team ministries, his strategy for the diocese wasn't remembered. It was Launcelot Fleming, the friend, who had left such an impression. Everyone had a story of a game of tennis played, a postcard received, a word of encouragement given, a lasting interest taken in their youthful well-being. For the people who remembered him had mostly been in their student years or their early 20s at the time of his ministry. Although Launcelot married Jane Agutter during his time as Bishop of Norwich, he arrived as a bachelor bishop, having previously been Bishop of Portsmouth. The routines he established at Bishop's House meant that he often entertained young people for lunch or supper and took them for a brisk walk around the garden. His network of contacts was immense and he shaped many lives by taking young people seriously and believing they could achieve great things.

Launcelot Fleming had been Dean of Trinity Hall. He had presided at Robert Runcie's marriage to Lindy Turner. Robert Runcie kept a photograph of Launcelot alongside one of Eric Abbot, former Dean of Westminster, at Lambeth Palace. They were two priests of enormous influence on the twentieth-century Church of England.

Many priests of Launcelot's generation were warned off making friends with parishioners or students. 'Particular friendships' were thought to be especially dangerous to Christian ministry and to be avoided as much in a parish as in a religious community. Yet Jesus speaks of his disciples as friends: 'You are my friends if you do what I command you ... love one another as I have loved you' (John 15.14, 17).

In his early life, Launcelot Fleming was an Antarctic explorer and he retained an expertise and interest in this area for the rest of his days. He belonged to a generation to whom ordination in the Church of England was not seen to be narrowing one's interests, sympathies or participation in the life of the body politic. Ordination united the adventure of faith with the wider adventure of life. So it was no surprise in his later days as a bishop in the House of Lords that he played such a significant role in the continuation of the British Antarctic Survey. It never occurred to him that science and faith inhabited different worlds or were in opposition to one another. Life was whole as well as holy.

When I preached at the Commemoration of the Benefactors service at Trinity Hall in 2000, a succession of elderly men trooped out of the Chapel, many of them saying to me, 'I was one of Launcelot's lambs'. Thus were they known, though without any of the sinister insinuation which such a term may suggest in our own age. For Launcelot

129

was perhaps the last of the Edwardians (it was the age in which he was born) for whom intimate friendship between men was not simply possible but desirable. The language of love was then used more freely in relation to same sex friendships than it seems to be now when we honour and celebrate same sex partnerships. Our tendency to see homoeroticism in all same sex affection would have stunted the capacity for the sort of Christian ministry Launcelot Fleming exercised so remarkably. It is a grievous loss.

One of the most surprising things in the New Testament is to find Jesus describing the disciples as his friends. He was their Master and their Lord. Disciples are followers. These days, celebrities, pop singers and film stars don't simply have followers but fans. It is intriguing that we customarily shorten the word fanatic in this way, since we still see fanatics as dangerous people. And for good reason – blind loyalty is dangerous.

Perhaps that is one of the reasons why Jesus chooses to call his disciples 'friends'. It isn't blind loyalty he wants or desires. But in calling them friends he redefines friendship too. We often gain a great deal from friendship. It is a two-way process, rewarding on both sides. A true friendship isn't possible if one of the pair is uninterested. Friendship dies without mutuality.

What need had Jesus for his disciples to be his friends? What need had he for friends at all? None in the sense that there was anything defective in his humanity which only human friendship could remedy. In John's gospel the passages about friendship redefine it and enlarge its character.

One of the problems of human friendship is exclusivity. It is one of the reasons why clergy have often been told not to become friends with parishioners. It seems to be divisive. When we make a good friend we can become jealous of their wider friendships. We sometimes dislike our friends making new friends. Possessiveness is corrosive. That is why close friends sometimes keep new friendships hidden from their existing friends. But this leads to compartmentalized and less truthful lives.

Jesus offers his friendship unconditionally when he 'shows the full extent of his love' (John 13.1). He will lay down his life for his friends (John 15.13), but he is not to be possessed as a friend. Even in the first resurrection appearance he tells Mary Magdalene 'do not cling to me' (John 20.17). The friendship the risen Christ has with those who share life with him on the road to Emmaus or over the breakfast he cooks for them is not exclusive. It's a friendship to be shared. That is the experience of Christians when receiving the sacrament of Holy Communion. We cannot hold on to him, clutching him only to ourselves. We are to discover him in others, not least those kneeling beside us. We cannot cherish Christ if we reject his presence in the Body of Christ, those whom he has chosen to be his friends, sometimes people we would never have chosen for ourselves. The mystery of friendship in Christ is that it is both gift and sacrifice.

Christ our companion, put away our possessiveness, enlarge our sympathies and broaden our appreciation of those you count as your friends within the fellowship of your Body, the Church. Amen.

19

All Things to All People
Robert Runcie

1 Corinthians 9.19–23

When I last spoke to Robert Runcie on the telephone, he was due to give the address at a memorial service for Peter Moore, sometime Dean of St Albans, the following day. Fastidious as ever, he tried out some of the content of his sermon on me. Had he got it right? Did he do Peter justice?

Robert delivered that address seated. His prostate cancer was very advanced indeed. Very soon after he got home he was barely conscious. Within a couple of days he had died.

Many words have been written about Robert Runcie. Three biographies and two substantial books of essays are a tribute to the impact he made. Much ink has been spent on the great events of Robert's archiepiscopate. These included the first ever papal visit to Britain, the sermon he preached after the

Falklands War and the controversy which followed it, as well as the publication of *Faith in the City* and the hostility it received from some government ministers. Then there was the work of Terry Waite as the Archbishop's envoy negotiating the release of hostages in different parts of the world. (The term envoy was largely the creation of the media. Terry was Secretary for Anglican Communion Affairs at Lambeth Palace.) Most of what has been written about Robert has said little of his inner life. That's partly the product of a proper reserve characteristic of Robert's generation. He was reserved about his war service too. The experience of the battlefield seems to make the sensitive spirit go deep.

The story of his last address, for a friend and colleague with whom he did not always agree, was characteristic of the priest and archbishop I knew. He gave himself fully and completely to his ministry and to the vocation to which he was called. Even when so enfeebled physically by his cancer, he gave priority to someone else and believed only the best would do. He set himself high standards and was always anxious to get things right.

I became his chaplain at Lambeth Palace in September 1987. A couple of months later the controversy following the publication of the preface to *Crockford's Clerical Directory* erupted. This anonymous commentary on Church affairs was always written from an insider's perspective. It was witty, well-crafted and malicious about the Archbishop. To the Archbishop himself, and those of us who worked with him, it was very clearly the work of Gareth Bennett from New College Oxford, a Church historian of some distinction but much frustrated by a lack of preferment. After a media frenzy to find the anonymous writer, Gareth Bennett killed himself. It was a tragedy at every level. It was also harrowing for Robert Runcie to live through this period. He never spoke of the matter in public and maintained a quiet dignity. He continued with his impossibly full diary of commitments, never giving any public impression of being distracted. He emerged with his reputation enhanced. Robert's ability to attend to those whom he met and to focus on them was not simply a pastoral skill. It derived from secure devotional routines. Morning Prayer, often followed by the Eucharist, in Lambeth Palace Chapel provided one of the foundations of Robert's ministerial life. It was one of the sources for the spiritual rhythm for his ministry. On a daily basis it was also where he was ministered to. Others led the services. The Archbishop was on the receiving end of grace. He knew how to receive, so he knew how to give.

Robert was a man surprisingly detached from material possessions, although he appreciated good things when he saw them. He possessed an aesthetic eye. He knew a fine wine from a bottle of plonk. He had taste, but there was something spare about him. He did not need much, perhaps a consequence of his wartime experience. Tank commanders get their priorities right. If you have a capacity to give yourself away you don't need to hold on to very much. None of us can hold on to anything as we pass from this life to the next. Christian spirituality is about learning to live in preparation for the next world as well as being fully committed to this one. Giving ourselves to others enhances our experience of human life. It's also a training ground for heaven.

Robert Runcie was born on Merseyside in 1921. He did not come from a devout family but caught the faith at St Faith's, Great Crosby and at Merchant Taylors' School. Service in the Scots Guards followed by a degree in Greats at Brasenose College, Oxford, gave people the impression that he came from a more privileged background than was really the case. He scarcely ever referred to his Military Cross. His wartime service and experience as one of the first to enter the Belsen concentration camp meant he knew the fragility of life, and how tragically human beings destroy it. His reaction to war was not to reject the image of God found in human beings but to treasure their foibles, eccentricities and dignity the more. His was an incarnational faith. Jesus Christ living among us and within us was the ground of his compassion. His humour was connected to his faith and spirituality, a sign of transcendence and humility. Robert was keen to point out that 'people with no sense of humour shouldn't be put in charge of anything'.

In the *Crockford's* preface, one of the criticisms made of Robert Runcie was that 'he nailed his colours firmly to the fence'. It was a surprising charge for someone whose archiepiscopate was so controversial. He did not endorse the dominant political philosophy of his day – Thatcherism. He supported Desmond Tutu and the Anglican Church in South Africa when the prevailing political leadership in Britain still described the African National Congress as a terrorist organization. Despite this, there was a sense in which Robert did seem to be all things to all people. But so did St Paul: 'I have become all things to all people, so that I might by any means save some. I do it all for the sake of the Gospel' (1 Corinthians 9.22–23).

In my address at Robert Runcie's funeral I remarked that it is odd that this missionary virtue should be looked upon with suspicion in our own day. St Paul became all things to all people through conviction, not uncertainty. He said that 'to the weak I became weak so that I might win the weak … to the Jews I became a Jew in order to win Jews' (1 Corinthians 9.22; 9.20). To the Corinthians, St Paul spoke of the Church as the body of Christ in a city where the human body was the source of peaks of sensual excitement. Paul risked being misunderstood. But he chose an image which related to the experience of the people he addressed in order to draw them to faith in Jesus Christ. That was the Runcie way too. Not that Robert and St Paul were the same in everything. Robert Runcie was tall and St Paul tells us he was short in stature. In other ways, though, they had more in common than many would imagine.

> *Incarnate Lord, lead us so to identify with others that we may become all things to all people for the sake of the Gospel. And in doing so, give us such a sense of proportion that you may make us channels of your grace and peace. Amen.*

20

Uncovenanted Mercies
Kathleen Ferrier

Romans 12.9–13

When I was about six or seven years old, my parents bought a gramophone. They couldn't afford many records, so the ones we did possess were played endlessly. The very first to be heard on this remarkable new machine was a recording of Kathleen Ferrier singing 'What is Life?', an operatic aria by Gluck. Along with the hymns sung in church, it formed part of the foundation of my musical education. Kathleen Ferrier was as near to a pop star as my parents felt able to admire. I now wonder if they knew much about her. She sang sacred songs like an angel, possessed a radiant personality, and died young, aged only 41, in October 1953, as a result of breast cancer. She had the lustre of a glorious life tragically ended too soon. She was adored by the British public at the time.

Within a few years of my parents buying that

gramophone I was purchasing records myself to play on it. None included sacred music. The pop charts claimed my attention. Yet the haunting sound of Kathleen Ferrier singing 'Blow the Wind Southerly' or 'What is Life?' occupies a surprisingly vibrant place in my musical memory. The more I have learned of her the more intriguing she seems to be, not least in relation to the gifts of the Spirit found in ordinary human lives where faith in God is barely acknowledged.

Kathleen was born in 1912 in Lancashire, the daughter of a village schoolteacher who then became a headmaster in Blackburn when she was just two years old. It was a family which enjoyed music and was sufficiently middle class for piano lessons to be arranged for Kathleen. She sang in a school choir but her voice was so powerful she was asked to tone it down. So she concentrated on the piano instead and proved herself a highly competent accompanist.

Kathleen left school at the age of 14 and worked as a telephonist for the Post Office. She loved dancing as well as music. Albert Wilson, a dance partner and a young bank branch manager, became her husband in 1933. She knew this was probably a mistake even before the marriage, but could not bring it to an end. They had little in common. What was worse was that the Post Office would not then employ married women, so Kathleen lost her job. Albert preferred her to be at home in any case. But there were no children to look after. It seems that the marriage was never consummated. Even on their honeymoon it became clear that they were physically unsuited.

A turning point in Kathleen's life came in 1937. She had entered the piano competition in the Carlisle Festival. Wondering whether to venture into the singing competition for contralto soloists as well, she said, 'I was still toying with the idea when my husband bet me a shilling I wouldn't do so. That clinched the matter and I entered winning first prize and the rose bowl for the best singer in the Festival'. We all owe a lot to Albert's dismissive remark. After this, Kathleen's career began to take off, at first locally and in the wider North-West, and then nationally once the Second World War began.

Kathleen was recruited by the Centre for the Encouragement of Music and the Arts (CEMA) and sent all over England and Wales to sing in factories, church halls and community centres. It was all done to boost war morale and enhance the cultural life of working people. Kathleen was energetic and captivating. Sir Malcolm Sergeant was impressed by her and suggested she ought to move to London if she really wanted to make her mark. In 1942 she did so, and with her sister Winifred she lived in a flat in Hampstead. She received specialist singing lessons from Professor Roy Henderson, a renowned singing teacher. Kathleen played the role of Lucretia in Benjamin Britten's new opera *The Rape of Lucretia*. She travelled across Europe after the war ended and undertook four North American tours as well. Everywhere she went she found new friends and admirers. She packed an enormous amount into the single decade during which she was prominent in the public eye.

Kathleen's marriage was dissolved in 1947, though it had really ended when war broke out. Ronald Duncan, who wrote the libretto for the *The Rape of Lucretia*, came to know Kathleen well. While everyone thought of Kathleen as vivacious, fun and almost carefree, she said to him that 'searching through hell for love is something I do all the time'. Referring to flowers sent to her after one of her performances, she remarked that 'these orchids have been sent to my voice … but I wish someone would pick one daisy for me'. Lucretia made her wreath from orchids, so the reference may be deeper than it first seems. More than once Kathleen referred to her bed as 'my virgin couch'.

Despite the zest for life so evident in her surviving letters, there seems a deep lack of fulfilment in her own emotional life. Even so, her character and personality conveyed a spiritual depth reflected in the comments of many distinguished people when Kathleen died. Sir John Barbirolli (one of her great mentors) observed that 'She had an almost startling simplicity'. Gerald Moore spoke of 'her example of nobility and humility, her stunning beauty and grace, her goodness and truth'. She struck Bruno Walter as 'pure and earnest, simple and noble'. He said she was not 'enigmatic nor problematic, but a rare combination of profundity and clarity ... an uncomplicated mind ... a country lass and a priestess'. It's intriguing that he used that last word in days before it had any pejorative sense. She mediated grace. It was Archbishop William Temple who once said that there are some souls for whom it seems to be necessary that they should die young. Some people thought of Keats or Shelley in that way. Kathleen Ferrier may be added to the pantheon.

A great deal of the music which inspired her was religious. Yet Kathleen (according to her sister) seldom, if ever, discussed religion and had no connection of any sort with any church, religious tradition or denomination. There was scarcely

143

anything of the orthodox Christian about her. I'm sure my parents did not realize this at all, nor did many of the other religious people of her generation who so admired her. Kathleen never received any sacraments, nor seemed to feel the need of them.

Canon Roger Lloyd, writing in *The Spectator* in 1956, pondered all this in relation to Kathleen Ferrier's life. He turned Kathleen's extraordinary capacity to convey a grace-filled life into a more general and tantalizing reflection on holiness:

> There is an ancient problem which has always perplexed faithful Christians. Why do so many people who neglect all the recognised means of grace yet show all the signs of it? The only possible answer is to use the theological phrase and say that they are among God's uncovenanted mercies. It may be that life is not intended to be so perfectly mapped that every event and every person falls neatly into place, and the whole picture is a limpid clarity. The divine purpose in a life like hers may be to keep the rest of us humble and make us rejoice; humble, because it eludes our classification and we cannot explain it. And rejoicing because it is a gift which lights up our

paths. She cannot be thought of without thanking God, and that is what is basic in sanctity.

Not to be able to think of someone without thanking God. That's an indication of a life mediating grace. An uncovenanted mercy.

Mysterious God, you fill with your grace
the lives of many people who do not seem
to acknowledge you; ensure we share your
generosity and make us glad to behold your
uncovenanted mercies. Amen.

21

The Architect of Salvation
John Loughborough Pearson

1 Peter 2.4–10

When I lived with my family in south London in the late 1980s and early 1990s we worshipped regularly at St Peter's, Vauxhall. At the time, St Peter's had a small congregation of widely different nationalities and backgrounds. Among the 30 or so communicants at the parish mass you would perhaps find a student from Cameroon, a family originally from Sri Lanka, Sisters of the Community of St John the Divine (now made famous through the television series *Call the Midwife*), one or two Jamaicans, a handful of locals who had lived all their lives in Vauxhall and a cabinet minister with a constituency in the Home Counties who was a regular worshipper. The diversity of the congregation expanded as the numbers gradually grew. It was a rewarding congregation to which to preach. It also provided some parochial reality given the rarefied atmosphere of working at Lambeth Palace at the time. The north Lambeth clergy were very welcoming to various clerical cuckoos in their nest. Over the years, Christopher Hill and Stephen Platten also ministered at St Peter's while they worked for the Archbishop of Canterbury. All three of us later became diocesan bishops. St Peter's comes to mind when pondering the needs of urban churches which face financial challenges or struggle to find lay people to do all the jobs which keep the Church going.

The architecture of St Peter's, Vauxhall, soon cast a spell on me. Built in 1864, it was designed by John Loughborough Pearson. He had already created a number of other buildings in the Gothic style in the streets nearby. He was commissioned to do so by Robert Gregory, who became Rector of Lambeth in 1853. Shocked by the penury of his people, the new rector quickly opened a drawing school in the parish room. He followed this with a new school designed by Pearson and built on part of the old Vauxhall Gardens. An art school was soon added and gained great renown. A soup kitchen and a clothes workshop followed. Poor women were paid 1s 6d a day for making clothes. They were so proficient that the government army clothing department put in massive orders. In one year alone 100,000 shirts were produced as well as several thousand greatcoats. It was Robert Gregory's vision to give the people of the parish paid work, to enhance their skills and education so that they might live a more elevated and purposeful life. Only then would they be able to glimpse the glory of God. He asked Pearson to build a suitable church for the people. It had to be a cheap church, but uplifting. Somehow St Peter's, which cost £8,000, not a vast sum even then for a church built on its scale, succeeds in transporting worshippers into another world as soon as they enter the door, the gate of heaven.

St Peter's is the first of Pearson's churches to be vaulted throughout its entire length. He claimed to be able to produce a vault as cheaply as any ordinary roof. It was an extraordinary achievement. With the roofline unbroken, the emphasis in the nave, chancel and sanctuary is on the vertical. Pearson's churches seem even higher than they are because side aisles are narrower than usual and side chapels often lower. Pearson's churches combine majesty and grace out of theological conviction and not simply architectural principle. He believed, like Robert Gregory, that true human dignity was found both in the worship of God and in work and education which enhanced life.

John Loughborough Pearson was born in 1817 in Brussels, though he spent his formative years in Durham. While his architectural practice was not limited to churches alone, he was at his most inspired in designing religious buildings. It gave him an opportunity to express his faith. He was just 16 when the Oxford Movement began. A growing number of priests and lay people in the Church of England became convinced about its Catholic character. The Gothic style was thought to be the architectural form most appropriate for conveying Christian and Catholic truth. Until we worshipped at St Peter's, Vauxhall, my own ministry had been spent entirely in twentieth-century churches with rather undistinguished architecture. My formation as a Christian had been in nonconformity where the plainness of a church interior was reflected in equally plain worship. At St Peter's, Vauxhall, I regularly presided and worshipped within a church building which was itself sacramental. St Peter's was a means of grace, a place in which it was easy to pray. I sensed what Robert Gregory and J. L. Pearson sought to provide for the people of Vauxhall. It was not gilded decoration or expensive materials which spoke of the glory of God. It was soaring vaulting which lifted the spirit and created a sense of one's own smallness when faced with the majesty of God. Little wonder that Anglo-Catholicism had such an impact in the poor parishes of London in the latter half of the nineteenth century. Pearson described his ambition in designing a church interior as one to bring people 'soonest to their knees'. He achieved just that.

Robert Gregory's huge Lambeth parish got divided up. In 1860, prior to St Peter's being completed, a new parish of Vauxhall was created. The rather appropriately named George W. Herbert became its first vicar. He served his poor parish for 34 years. Altar lights, Eucharistic vestments, sacramental confession and eventually the regular use of incense and a daily mass all became characteristic features of St Peter's, as in other Anglo-Catholic churches. The tradition, with some variation, continues to this day.

Two years before St Peter's was completed, J. L. Pearson married Jemima Christian, a cousin of the architect Ewan Christian who restored many churches in his own career, often rather severely. Within a month or two of St Peter's consecration, the only child of the marriage, Frank, was born. The following year Jemima died of typhoid fever. Happiness and sorrow followed each other very rapidly in Pearson's life. Architectural historians note a greater freedom in Pearson's architecture from the building of St Peter's onwards. The highly correct Gothic of his earlier years no longer restricted him. He became more inventive.

A change certainly took place. It is intriguing that this happened just at the time of the greatest tragedy in Pearson's adult life – the death of his young wife. The transition is not one which led to darkness. Pearson's later churches dance with even more light and offer perspectives which suggest new vistas as one progresses through the buildings. Pearson was himself brought 'soonest to his knees' not by architecture but by grief. He rose, eventually, with new purpose and fired by gratitude for his marriage and for the gift of his son, who eventually succeeded him in his architectural practice. Pearson walked the way of the Cross. He found in it a freedom which sustained him. The personal tragedy he suffered seemed to lead him to even greater delicacy of design, combining the majesty and tenderness of God.

On leaving St Peter's, Vauxhall, in 1993 I returned to my home county of Cornwall as Bishop of St Germans. My new ministry began in Truro Cathedral, one of Pearson's greatest buildings. I had known it for years but now saw it in a new way. It did bring me 'soonest to my knees' as I prayed for grace to sustain me in my episcopal ministry. I imagined John Loughborough Pearson kneeling there too. I gave thanks for this great architect who, through stone and wood, created such great sacramental buildings in honour of him who wielded the tools of a carpenter's workshop, the architect of our salvation.

Great architect of our salvation, fashion us as living stones witnessing to your grace, and bring us soonest to our knees first in penitence and then in gratitude for your undeserved forgiveness. Amen.

22

Seeing God

Edith James

Matthew 20.29–34

My maternal grandmother, Edith James[1], became totally blind as a result of glaucoma shortly before I was born. It was a needless tragedy since even then it was a treatable condition. But help was sought too late. Edith spent some time in a psychiatric hospital as she came to terms with her new and restricted life. St Lawrence's Hospital in Bodmin was feared in Cornwall in the 1940s, partly the result of the social stigma of mental illness, but also for the sheer unpleasantness of what was still known as an asylum.

Edith died when I was just 14, but she had a profound influence upon me. To spend your early years so often in the company of a blind person gave me some insight into living with disability. Although she had had no more than a rudimentary education in the closing years of Queen Victoria's reign, she always gave the impression of being a more educated person than was actually the case. She was definitely more cultured than one might have expected. As I look back I believe this was because she had a grace which was refined by suffering. Hers was a simple yet profound Methodist faith which still bore the marks of the 'scriptural holiness' which John Wesley wanted to spread throughout the land.

Among my earliest memories is one of my grand-mother wanting to 'see what I looked like' by touching my face. Whether that was really an aid to her imagination I am not sure, but she became strong on touch as a means of human connection. Jesus welcomed children physically by taking them in his arms and blessing them. It was a sign of God's acceptance of them: 'Unless you become like a little child, you will not enter the kingdom of heaven'. Blindness was then thought to be the result of sin, whether of the blind person herself or a conse-quence of her forbears' wickedness. When Jesus touched blind people he indicated their acceptance before God and aided their integration into society. He did not wait for repentance. It was God's initi-ative in healing, mercy and love that was on display. The touch of Jesus was neither sentimental nor only a means of physical healing. It was a celebration of full humanity. No wonder Edith felt such a devotion to the person of Jesus.

Ours is a society fearful of touch, especially of children by strangers, and for good reason. But it is an impoverishment to deny ourselves a ministry of touch. I realize how much my grandmother's life and full humanity depended upon her touching others and being touched herself.

Edith's life became very restricted after blindness took hold of her. She rarely left her extremely modest home, set on the main road between Redruth and Camborne in Cornwall. She never had a white stick nor grew confident enough to venture out alone. Perhaps that's the consequence of becoming blind later in life, though I realize now that she was no more than 50 years of age when her sight failed her. She always seemed much much older.

I must have been only eight or nine when I was walking with my grandmother on one of her relatively rare days out on a Cornish cliff top. My parents and the rest of the family would have been there but I remember my grandmother holding my arm. I realized even at my young age that she had placed her full trust in me to keep her to the path, to prevent her from stumbling or missing her step. I felt suddenly adult. I don't suppose I explained it to myself then in such a way but I did feel a strong sense of responsibility for my grandmother's well-being. I loved her and did not want her to come to any harm. Because she trusted me so fully, I felt an even greater love towards her. It taught me something about the nature of God's love. Does our trust in him mean that he loves us more? God's love can scarcely be dependent on our fickle response. But our sense of God's love for us does increase the more we place our trust in him. Trust and love go together. The connection between my trust in God and God's love for me has been one of the firmest convictions of my life. Upon that my Christian faith is grounded. It has been the foundation of my ministry to others. I realize now how much I owe this to my grandmother Edith.

Pope Francis has spoken of the importance of grandparents to young people and how we should treasure their role more in the formation of the young. His words struck true with me. For Pope Francis it was his Grandma Rosa who taught him Italian (she came originally from Piedmont) and who also taught him to pray and told him stories of the saints. He spent a great deal of time with her as a young boy, and wonders what she makes of her grandson becoming Pope from wherever she is in the heavenly places.

My grandmother didn't teach me to pray but I was aware she prayed for me (though there wasn't a trace of false piety in her). For Edith it was Charles Wesley's hymns and Moody and Sankey[2] evenings that were the core devotional material of her faith.

Her life was limited, her means were modest, and her disabilities increased as she aged. By the time she was in her early 70s she had become very deaf as well as blind. Yet she smiled a lot, and had great serenity. She thanked God for his blessings. I was dimly aware that my older brother and I, her only grandchildren, were reckoned to be among the blessings for which God deserved gratitude.

Pope Francis's Grandma Rosa had fewer physical constraints with which to cope but she had little of this world's goods too. She wrote a note for her grandchildren which Pope Francis is said to keep in his breviary. It says this:

> May, these, my grandchildren, to whom I
> gave the best my heart has to offer, have
> long and happy lives, but if some day

159

sorrow, sickness or the loss of a beloved
person should fill them with distress,
let them remember that a sigh directed
towards the tabernacle, home to the
greatest and noblest martyr, and a look to
Mary at the foot of the cross, can drop a
soothing balm on the deepest and most
painful of wounds.

It was popular Catholic piety which shaped, formed and refined the life of Pope Francis's grandmother. It was popular Methodist piety which did the same for my grandmother Edith. She relied on the touch of Jesus Christ on her life for blessing and reassurance. Her emotions and her spirit were touched by the marks of popular devotion too. Hers was a grace-filled life. 'Heaven in ordinary,' George Herbert would have said.

*Lord Jesus Christ, you touched the eyes of the
blind, restore our vision so that we may see
you more clearly and be transformed by your
refining grace. Amen.*

Notes

1   My mother's maiden name was James. Two separate
    families of Jameses came together when my parents
    married. It took me quite a while as a child to

understand that not all families had the same surname throughout.

2   Ira Sankey and Dwight Moody wrote evangelical and revivalist hymns and songs and travelled widely in the United States and Great Britain in the closing decades of the nineteenth century. They drew great crowds and touched the hearts of many working people.

23

The Mind of the Maker
Dorothy L Sayers

1 John 5.6–13

Lord Peter Wimsey, the aristocratic sleuth, never captured my imagination or affection but his creator, Dorothy L. Sayers, certainly did. She deserves to be remembered as one of the great Christian apologists of the twentieth century. Her radio series *The Man Born to be King* drew huge audiences and some controversy. But her most enduring work is *The Mind of the Maker*, which illuminated the truth of the doctrine of the Holy Trinity for me as no sermon or other essay in apologetics has ever done.

Dorothy Sayers was born in 1893, an only child. Her father was a priest and headmaster of Christ Church Cathedral School in Oxford. When Dorothy was four the family moved to a rather bleak Fenland parish in Cambridgeshire, which had the compensation of a large endowment. Her father was paid

£1,500 per annum to look after a few hundred parishioners. This he did conscientiously though it seems much of the pastoral work was undertaken by Dorothy's mother, Helen. Dorothy experienced the irritation that only children often have towards their parents, but her affection for them and her childhood home is reflected in the fictional Fenland setting of one of her most popular novels, *The Nine Tailors*. Anglican clergy are sympathetically described in Sayers' work, a tribute to her fondness for her father who loved his daughter intensely and loved music and his books almost as well. He doesn't seem to have been an exciting man since Dorothy wrote after his death, 'He bored mother to death for nearly forty years, and she always grumbled that he was no companion for her – and now she misses him dreadfully'.

Dorothy Sayers' own personal and domestic life was anything but dull and boring. She fell hopelessly in love with an American writer, John Cournos, who eventually rejected her. Cournos was rather affected and Dorothy idealized him. After this rejection, Dorothy became pregnant by a man whom she had no desire at all to marry. She gave birth to her son, John Anthony, in January 1924 without telling her parents or anyone else, but persuaded her cousin and friend Ivy Shrimpton (who had been looking after orphan children) to take her infant son into her care. A few days before she was due to bring her son, John Anthony, to Ivy, Dorothy Sayers told Ivy the full story – or at least as much of it as she was willing to tell. Ivy kept the confidence intact and accepted what had happened and provided a home and security for Dorothy's son.

Two years later, in 1926, Dorothy married Oswald Fleming, a divorced journalist in his mid-40s and in poor health. His career was on the way down as Dorothy's soared. It looks as if she found him an uncomplicated person who would take John Anthony into their home. But her husband never agreed to this, and the marriage did not prosper. What is extraordinary is that Dorothy Sayers' closest friends never knew of her son's existence until after her death in 1957. Only those who were her personal secretaries (and were involved in sending cheques for John Anthony's support) as well as his teachers were aware of the truth. This must have been mental and spiritual torture for someone like Dorothy Sayers, who became a leading advocate of the Christian faith as lived in the Church of England during the latter half of her life. Perhaps all this explains why Dorothy had such a strong sense of her sinfulness. In a letter written in 1940 she said:

"... the story of a Crucified God appears irrelevant because people nowadays have no sense of sin ... I am a very poor person to appreciate modern man's feelings on all this, because I can't think of any personal misfortunes that have befallen me which were not, in one way or another, my own fault ... anything I have to put up with looks to me like the direct punishment of my *own* sins ... but I do see that most people today look upon themselves as the victims of undeserved misfortune, which they ... have done nothing to provoke."

It is sometimes claimed that Dorothy Sayers' emotional turmoil was the reason why her approach to Christianity was so resolutely intellectual. It wasn't because she lacked an emotional life. She wouldn't have got into such trouble with men if that had been the case. She was wonderfully entertaining, bawdy, witty and irreverent. She was intolerant of the lukewarm wherever she encountered it in life or in faith. She was captivated by Jesus Christ and the drama of his life, death and resurrection. She believed him to be the truth, not her truth or your truth, but *the* truth.

This conviction was expressed in her introduction

to *The Mind of the Maker*. She described it as 'a commentary, in the light of specialised knowledge, on a particular set of statements made in the Christian creeds and their claim to be statements of fact'. As statements of fact she meant the truth. She did not believe her book to be 'an expression of personal religious belief' and she felt she needed to make this clear 'for the popular mind has grown so confused that it is no longer able to receive any statement of fact except as an expression of personal feeling'.

The Mind of the Maker explored the Trinitarian character of all creative activity. The Creative Idea is the artist's vision of a picture or an author's conception of her work. It is the image of the Father. The Creative Energy is the work involved in putting paint on a canvas or writing the words. This is the Idea working in time with matter. It is the image of the incarnate word, the Son. Third, there is the Creative Power, which is communicated through the painting or the novel and evokes a response. This is the image of the Holy Spirit. Each is the whole creative work in itself and yet each is united with the other, a trinity in unity. If all that is true of creativity in the human world, is it not simply a reflection of the character of creation itself?

The Mind of the Maker is the most substantial theological legacy from Dorothy Sayers. Yet it was not this book but her series of plays, *The Man Born to be King*, which caused William Temple, the Archbishop of Canterbury, to offer her a Lambeth degree. He considered that the plays had been 'one of the most powerful instruments in evangelism which the Church has had put into its hands for a long time past'. So he wanted her to receive a Lambeth doctorate in divinity, pointing out that she would have been the first woman to do so. She hesitated, and then refused. For someone who enjoyed receiving honours and attending unusual ceremonies, this seems to have been a strange example of self-denial. One of her biographers thought it indicated the depth of the doubts with which she lived. More likely she was burdened by a sense of sin. The Archbishop pointed out that receiving a Lambeth degree was not a certificate of sanctity. But John Anthony was in her mind. Dorothy Sayers knew that the media of the time might take a greater interest in her personal life if she was honoured in this way.

We live in an age which often sees a sense of sin and guilt as incapacitating. Not for Dorothy L. Sayers. She did not seek God as a balm for her feelings. The liberation of her mind in God's truth gave her an exhilaration and a freshness in communicating her Christian conviction which has travelled well into a new century.

Author of life, we praise you for the work of creative writers and artists; feed our imaginations, forgive our shortcomings and take our modest gifts and use them for your good purposes. Amen.

24

Restlessness

George Borrow

Acts 17.22–28

The signs greeting drivers and other travellers crossing the boundary into the city of Norwich proclaim it 'A fine city'. It is, but few seem to know the origin of the phrase. George Borrow said this of the city where his family settled.

George Borrow was born in East Dereham in 1803. His father was a captain in the West Norfolk Militia. This meant a peripatetic family life, which may explain George's later love of travel, a good deal of it on foot. He spent three years at Norwich School. There George discovered a considerable gift for learning and speaking languages. His capacity to do so was not only the result of work in the classroom. He also discovered Romany culture. Gypsies and tinkers lived on Mousehold Heath, very near the centre of the city. Just outside the Cathedral gate and very near Norwich School, there were frequent fairs in the early part of the nineteenth century which gypsies helped to organize. George became proficient in the Romany tongue and became very friendly with these travelling people. His father, perhaps concerned that his unusual son might run away with them, found a job for him as a solicitor's clerk. He was quickly bored. When he was 21, he went to London to seek his fortune as a translator.

George did find work but there wasn't much money translating books from Danish, German and Spanish. So he ran off with the gypsies after all. He stored up his experience of living alongside the Romany travellers and drew on it to write novels which were published a decade or more later.

In the early 1830s, George Borrow's luck changed. An introduction to the British and Foreign Bible Society led to a commission to translate the New Testament into Manchu, the court language in China. Borrow learned the language in six months and was then sent to St Petersburg (rather than China itself) to do the work. This and other Bible translations established his reputation in England. It was modest fame at the time, not that he was one to seek it. He felt himself to be a world citizen at a time when travel was arduous and testing.

He married a widow, Mary Clarke. They had no children of their own though there was a stepdaughter, Henrietta. George did not make an easy husband. He often went out for walks and his wife had little idea how long a walk would take. On one occasion it was three months before he returned. George Borrow was tall, with long hair, staring eyes and a fiery temperament. He referred to attacks of the horrors, when any capacity for civil conversation deserted him entirely. After Mary died in 1869, George lived at Oulton Broad where he had a long-standing feud with the local rector. It was said of George Borrow that he was only truly at ease with gypsies. They were always welcomed when they camped at waste land near his Oulton Broad cottage. It is hard to imagine that his neighbours cherished him much.

This difficult and solitary man would make an uncomfortable Lenten companion but you would discover new things in his company if you were willing to travel with him. As with many travellers, he may have been seeking his own true self without ever quite making a satisfactory discovery. From its earliest days Christianity has always been a religion on the move. The apostles were those who were sent out. Jesus may not have travelled very far but his band of fishermen, zealots and tax collectors were propelled into a world much wider than rural Galilee where they were recruited. It was Christianity on the move, rather than the Church as a settled institution, which appealed to George Borrow. No wonder that towards the end of his life he became interested in all things Celtic. The Celtic saints of Ireland, Wales, Cornwall and Brittany were great travellers with the Gospel.

There was a restlessness in George Borrow which challenges those of us who instinctively prefer stability and security and like the risks of life to be well-managed (and well insured). There is a proper restlessness in Christian discipleship. Here on earth 'we have no abiding city'. Borrow may have called Norwich a fine city but he did not want to stay there long. He would have been more likely to identify with St Augustine who began his *Confessions* by saying of God 'you have made us for yourself and our hearts are restless until they find their rest in you'.

George Borrow had a restless spirit. He was quirky and judgemental and possessed of a very serious bias against Catholicism. He responded poorly to all forms of authority. His relationship with the British and Foreign Bible Society was stormy. And yet many people came to read the scriptures as a result of his work as a Bible translator. It is estimated that he learned up to a hundred languages, at least to some degree. Was he seeking God or truth or simply wanting to discover himself? How far were his long walks around Wales, Scotland, Cornwall and the Isle of Man simply the result of his restless spirit?

George Herbert in his poem 'The Pulley' says God gave human beings every possible blessing except one – a restful spirit. There is something in us which is not entirely at peace in this world. If that were not the case we would never strive for God and have no longing for him. Herbert concludes his poem by wondering what would happen if we were to find the rest of which St Augustine speaks:

> For if I should (said he)
> Bestow this jewell also on my creature,
> He would adore my gifts instead of me,
> and rest in Nature, not the God of Nature
>
> So both should losers be.
> Yet let him keep the rest
> But keep them with repining restlessness:
> Let him be rich and wearie, that at least,
> If goodnesse leade him not, yet wearinesse
>   may tosse him to my breast.

175

Eternal God, we know our restlessness is a search for you and your peace; enliven us with enough longing to seek you and enough capacity to trust in you that we may rest our weary souls in your embrace. Amen.

25

God, Forever Young
Enid Ralphs

John 21.15–19

Enid Ralphs died just after her 99th birthday in January 2014. She came originally from Cornwall where she attended Penzance Grammar School for Girls, later returning to teach geography there. She was a student at Exeter University in the 1930s and became President of the Students' Union, and also Vice-President of the National Union of Students. She had great gifts of leadership. In 1938, Enid Cowlin (as she then was) married Lincoln Ralphs. He was to become a very notable Chief Education Officer in Norfolk and was knighted for his services to education in 1973. He died in 1978. Enid's widowhood was almost as long as her marriage.

They must have been a formidable couple. One of Lincoln's great schemes was to develop a state boarding school just after the Second World War, initially using Nissen huts near Wymondham. Wymondham College is now one of the jewels in the state boarding system, a feature of state education which might have passed away had it not been for champions like Lincoln and Enid Ralphs. She maintained a passionate interest in the well-being of Wymondham College to the very end of her life.

Enid Ralphs was an achiever. In 1981 she became the first woman to chair the Magistrates Association of England and Wales. She lectured part-time at the Keswick Hall College of Education in Norwich until her retirement in 1980 and was President of the Norwich branch of the United Nations Association as well as President of Norfolk Girl Guiding. A commitment to a peaceful, cooperative post-war world inspired her. The right administration of justice with compassion was a guiding principle. Enid possessed an abiding love of young people. Her own spirit was youthful and she had no time at all for generational boundaries, believing that the elderly had much to give to the young and much to learn from them too.

Not many people die at the age of 99 and still fill a great cathedral for their memorial service. Enid did. She had outlived the vast majority of her contemporaries, but continued to make friends, including young friends, well into her tenth decade. I've hardly met anyone less tempted by nostalgia than Enid. Given her achievements (and those of her husband with Enid alongside him) it would have been very easy indeed for her to think that educational provision, the life of the Church of England or contemporary morality had fallen below the high standards she once knew. As it was, I often found myself having to explain why the Church of England had failed to approve the legislation for women to become bishops or why we were not more forward-thinking in addressing the issues of our time. She was grateful for a life of huge activity but she never ceased to live in the present.

I think Enid's secret was really no secret at all. She had a deep and committed faith in Jesus Christ, through whom the love of God for her became a living reality. The imagery with which the Bible and the Christian tradition speaks of God often makes him sound aged and venerable. To describe God as the 'Ancient of Days' or even the 'Father Everlasting' suggests God has been around for a very long time indeed – even longer than our medieval parish churches. This weight of heritage associated not simply with the Church as an institution but with the image of God himself was precisely what in the

1960s Bishop John Robinson wanted to dethrone. When it was said 'our image of God must go', it was partly this leaden and constricting sense of aged imagery and unchanging formularies that was the problem. It was as if God's honour could only be protected if everything was passed on inviolate and preserved entirely in form and character from one generation to another.

Enid never saw God in this way at all. Her God was youthful in spirit, hopeful in action, just in his dealings with humankind, and endlessly compassionate.

Some years ago I attended a diocesan youth event. A good crowd of young people had gathered, but those in charge had decided that young people liked informality. In this case, informality meant disorganization. There were lots of good workshops, talented musicians and abundant ideas, but it was all rather chaotic. It was saved by the closing act of worship. A number of the young people had devised it themselves on the day. During the prayers they unfurled a banner which proclaimed 'God is forever young'.

The youthfulness of God. I'd never heard a sermon on the subject. I'd never really thought about it.

In so far as the ageing process means anything in relation to the eternal God, it became suddenly clear to me that the Ancient of Days was indeed 'forever young'. There was no dissonance between them.

One of the dangers of growing old is that we can become envious of the young. Seeing a young couple in love with all their life before them can hit a widow or widower hard. Experiencing a younger person promoted above you at work when you are still some years from retirement can lead to great heaviness of spirit. We don't all age gracefully. Sometimes the young remind us of potential in our lives which we have failed to fulfil.

In Jesus Christ we have a young saviour, although 33 was probably middle-age in Palestine at the time of his crucifixion. We need role models of gracious ageing, since the example of Methuselah[1] is not a great deal of help. You don't have to be very old to become nostalgic, to look back longingly. It is striking that in his resurrection appearances Christ makes no direct reference to his earlier ministry when he is with the disciples. There is no reminiscing about their shared experience travelling around Galilee. There is no looking back. The trajectory is into the future. There is just one exception, and even this contains no explicit reference to any past event. It is when Christ asks Simon Peter, 'Do you love me?' three times. He asks often enough for Peter to become indignant at the repetition. It was, of course, a way of forgiving Peter's earlier threefold denial that he even knew Jesus. Peter begins again. The Risen Christ leads his followers into a new adventure, a dangerous one for many of them.

Enid Ralphs lived for the future until the very end of her earthly life. As a preparation for what is to come, she lived well. She was forever young, like the God in whom she believed.

> *Eternal God, forever young and Ancient of Days, give us a right perspective on the past, joy in the present, and hope for the future, so that we may discern the signs of your coming Kingdom of justice, peace and love. Amen.*

Note

1 Genesis 5.27 records Methuselah as living for 969 years, the longest lifespan attributed to anyone in the Hebrew Bible.

26

Integrity and Justice

John Lyttle

John 16.12–15

John Lyttle gave the last four years of his life to the quest to secure the release of Terry Waite, taken hostage in Lebanon in January 1987. He never lived to see Terry's return to England, and so did not meet him. John joined the staff at Lambeth Palace as the Archbishop of Canterbury's Secretary for Public Affairs just when Terry left on his last ill-fated mission to the Middle East.

John was just 58 when he died and looked a good deal older. He lived on whisky and cigarettes and seemed to miss more meals than he ate. He needed to work for a cause in which he believed. He had been an effective Chief Secretary of the Race Relations Board before going on to become Political Adviser to Shirley Williams in 1974 when she was Secretary of State for Prices and Consumer Protection. That began a long association with her, and with other leading Labour figures, especially those who broke away to form the Social Democratic Party in 1981.

Many people were surprised when John became part of the Archbishop's staff at Lambeth Palace. An archiepiscopal court or personal household did not seem natural territory for someone disinclined to genuflect to institutions or those who represented them. Yet when he died John's obituaries in the press were warm, though they could have confused an unwary reader. One newspaper reported 'leading churchman dies'. Another began with the words 'Lyttle was not a religious man'. Perhaps only the Church of England, casting its net of sympathy so wide, may have recognized in John a leading churchman. But, in his own way, that's what he became. Often he spoke on behalf of the Church and the Archbishop about the hostage crisis, describing what he was seeking to do. He did not give away any unnecessary information or boast of his courage (it was a brave man who went to Lebanon and Iran in those days) and never raised unrealistic hopes. Journalists trusted and respected him. He was a reassuring figure to the Waite family. He took risks but was never taken in.

John was often a sceptic, but never a cynic. He had a natural suspicion of bureaucracies, committees and the motives of people who sought publicity for its own sake. His career gave his suspicious mind plenty of scope, but he was never dismissive of those who were genuinely victims of injustice, prejudice or bigotry. That was what made his service to the Race Relations Board so distinguished, particularly at a time when some still argued that the Race Relations Act was unnecessary. John was one of those people who helped to refashion public opinion.

It was his passion to oppose injustice, which meant he was able to give himself so unstintingly in his work for hostages, especially Terry. At John's funeral it was recognized that when Terry returned (and by then confidence was growing) it would be in no small measure due to the tireless work of this man Terry had never known.

John's demonology was well developed. His was a world which contained 'vipers', 'reptiles' and 'buffoons', but he never succumbed to the demonization of Middle Eastern people. The speed with which John's appreciation of the intricacies of Middle Eastern politics and religion grew over the final four years of his life was astounding. Journalists who had lived in the Middle East for years found their own understanding enlarged when they talked with him.

John Simpson, with a lifetime's experience working for the BBC in theatres of conflict, wrote about John when Terry Waite was finally released in November 1991. He said this:

> I thought of someone ... who worked and
> travelled tirelessly for this moment, yet
> died from the strain seven months before
> it arrived: John Lyttle, the Press Secretary
> [he was actually Secretary for Public
> Affairs] at Lambeth Palace. As I watched
> [Terry's speech on his return to England],
> I remembered all the pleasant sessions
> in John's office over a gin and tonic, the
> enigmatic phone calls about some obscure
> lead in Iran or Libya or Syria, the long
> walks between the flower beds in the Palace
> gardens in the summer before he died.
> There was great justice and great pleasure
> in watching Terry Waite being recalled ...
> to life. It was hard to see much of either in
> John Lyttle's untimely death.

John hated 'swirling words' being poured over people, so it is difficult to write anything about him more than two decades later without hearing his frequent admonitions. He may not have been devout in the accepted sense, but he was devoted

– to whatever cause he worked for, and to the people he served. He was a believer in the power of good to triumph over evil, in the capacity of honesty to conquer lies, in the ability of candour to expose dissembling. But his doctrine of redemption had limits. Once you were consigned to the realm of the 'batty' you were unlikely to be readmitted to the company of the sane.

In her autobiography *Climbing the Bookshelves*, Shirley Williams described how John excelled as a political adviser because he knew that a decision taken by a politician was never enough. It was the beginning of a process and not its end. She said he was a progress chaser, reporting to the Secretary of State on which policies were being energetically pursued, which were being obstructed by the civil servants and which were being left to wither on the vine. She wrote, 'nor was John inclined to tell one what one wanted to hear: the truth, however unwelcome, had to be told'. Shirley Williams then described what brought a lasting rift to their collaboration. John applied to be the new party's chief media officer, reckoning that since he had been so essential to the SDP's establishment and organization he would get the job. 'There was within him, however, an insistence on truth telling that eschewed compromise, a kind of whimsical obstinacy. Asked during his job interview what his strategy would be for television, John made his contempt for the medium clear. Television, unlike the printed press, did not interest him. It was a response that killed his chance of getting the job'.

Shirley Williams believed John never forgave her. Certainly the rift was never healed. But without it, he would never have worked for the Archbishop of Canterbury. The right person appeared there when Terry was captured.

John was the last person on whom to project faith. Yet he understood how the faith of others shaped their lives. He would sometimes make a surprise appearance at the community worship in Lambeth Palace Chapel. There was no chance that he would be there as a matter of form. In those final years of his life he began to discover why religious faith was such a motivating force in the lives of so many people in the world. He saw its dangers. He discovered too that God was not a tyrant to be obeyed but often drew the best out of stuttering, fragmented, mistake-making humanity. On one occasion during those years I travelled to Geneva with John to meet an Iranian contact. I was there at his request as witness, companion and rapporteur. John often seemed self-sufficient but he knew he couldn't do everything alone. It wasn't 'whimsical obstinacy' that I encountered. It was an extraordinary combination of courage and honesty with a growing vulnerability as he grew nearer to the release of the hostages and faced his own mortality too. That's why he was glad that other people had faith for him. Many of us as Christians respect and love such figures of integrity and leave it to God to determine whatever abundance of life he may give them.

> *God of integrity, keep us focused on justice*
> *and temper our rectitude with mercy.*
> *Strengthen all those imprisoned unjustly or*
> *who suffer for conscience sake and bless those*
> *who work for their release. Amen.*

27

Thanksgiving in Troubled Times
Edward Reynolds

Philippians 4.4–7

I was 11 when my family became Anglicans and I first encountered the Book of Common Prayer. There were only vestiges of liturgy in our Congregational worship, but we did frequently use the General Thanksgiving. As an eight- or nine-year-old I enjoyed getting my tongue around words like 'inestimable' and 'unfeignedly'. The General Thanksgiving is thus one of those prayers I can recite by heart very easily. As a child I did not know I was using a prayer written by Edward Reynolds, Bishop of Norwich after the Restoration of both the monarchy and episcopacy in 1660. Even less did I know I would one day succeed him. Few things would have seemed more unlikely to a Cornish Congregationalist child.

When my father was ordained in the Church of England, he became a curate in a Northampton parish. At one stage it seemed likely that he would go to All Saints, Northampton, though in the end he served at St John the Baptist, Kingsthorpe. All Saints, Northampton, was where Edward Reynolds had served as vicar in the 1620s. From my study window in Norwich I look out to the chapel Reynolds built and which is attached to the old Bishop's Palace. It was in this chapel that he was buried. Early in my time in Norwich I preached a series of sermons on 'the means of grace and hope of glory'. I realized just how deeply that phrase from the General Thanksgiving had embedded itself in my thinking and spirituality. Even so, I then knew very little about this man who had helped to shape my faith, and that of countless others, through this majestic prayer.

Edward Reynolds was born in Southampton but we know very little of his family. His education at the local grammar school was good enough for him to go as an exhibitioner to Merton College, Oxford, when he was just 16. He graduated when he was 19, became a fellow because of his ability in Greek, and was ordained at the minimum canonical age of 23. Remarkably he was then chosen to succeed John Donne as Preacher at Lincoln's Inn. Since his family seems to have been of little influence, this suggests a meteoric rise through ability alone. He appears to have held the living at All Saints, Northampton, alongside his employment at Lincoln's Inn, but when he became the incumbent at Braunston in Northamptonshire in 1631 he gave all his time to his pastoral and parochial ministry there.

Reynolds was no admirer of Archbishop Laud and what he believed to be an inappropriate attempt to make the liturgy of the Church of England more formal, emphasizing Catholic continuities rather than a Protestant reformed faith. Reynolds' sympathies were for a scriptural and disciplined life with the barest of rituals in church. He was not attracted to the use of the surplice, kneeling at communion or the use of the sign of the cross at baptism. While he had accepted episcopal orders and had no objection to a moderate episcopacy, he was equally able to recognize God at work within Presbyterian forms of church government. Reynolds was one of the Assembly of Divines who met at Westminster in June 1643 and compiled a larger and shorter catechism as well as a Confession of Faith which remains the standard teaching of the Church of Scotland. He wrote a very moderate preface to the new *Directory of Public Worship* which displaced the Book of Common Prayer. But he never believed the Book of Common

Prayer was idolatrous or unscriptural, nor did he ever believe himself to be anything other than the King's servant. He was rewarded for his faithful work with the Deanery of Christ Church, Oxford. However, he was eventually deprived in 1651 since he would not take the Statement of Engagement. This required all Church office holders to promise, 'I will be true and faithful to the Commonwealth of England as it is now established, without a King or House of Lords'.

As the Protectorate crumbled, Reynolds came to prominence again, preaching before Parliament in January 1657 then becoming vicar of St Lawrence Jewry in London before being restored to his Deanery at Christ Church in 1659. His sermons stressed the need for peace, unity and moderation. It was unmistakable that he was arguing for the Restoration of monarchy. He was one of five ministers to present an address on behalf of Parliament to Charles II at Breda, which prepared the ground for the Restoration. He became a chaplain to Charles II before becoming Bishop of Norwich where he gave his main attention to the needs of the diocese, the care of the clergy and preaching. Despite his involvement with the Restoration of the monarchy, he played little part later in affairs of state.

The puritan Richard Baxter described Reynolds as 'a solid honest man, but through mildness and excess of timorous deference to great men altogether unfit to contend with them'. Certainly Reynolds was no controversialist. Sir Thomas Browne, one of the great sons of the Diocese of Norwich, called him 'a divine of singular affability, meekness and humility, of great learning, and a frequent preacher'.

Reynolds and his colleagues had pressed for a more explicit expression of thanksgiving among some additional prayers added to the revised Book of Common Prayer, eventually published in 1662. It was written after a period of civil war, regicide, uncertainty and disruption. While Reynolds called his prayer 'A General Thanksgiving', the focus is on God's mercy. God is invoked as the 'Father of all mercies', and later a petition asks God to 'give us that due sense of all thy mercies' that our hearts may be unfeignedly thankful.

The mercy of God towards his world and his creatures is unfathomable. I remember a friend once saying of an extremely judgemental person, 'I am glad God is more merciful than X'. God is more merciful than any of us. Pope Francis has made God's mercy a leitmotif of his teaching. It generates a thankful heart.

In Luke's gospel, Jesus goes to the home of Simon the Pharisee for dinner. It is there that a woman with a bad reputation anoints his feet, washes them with her tears and dries them with her hair. A more highly charged and even erotic scene is scarcely to be imagined. No wonder Simon disapproves. And yet Jesus simply asks him a question: if a creditor had two debtors, one owing £500 and the other £50 and he cancelled the debts for them both, which of them would be more grateful? Simon thinks it will be the one who owed him the most. Mercy and thanksgiving are inseparable. That's why the General Thanksgiving is such a great prayer:

> Almighty God, Father of all mercies,
> We thine unworthy servants
> Do give thee most humble and hearty
>   thanks
> For all thy goodness and loving kindness
> To us and to all men
> We bless thee for our creation, preservation,
> And all the blessings of this life; but above
>   all for the inestimable love
> In the redemption of the world by our
>   Lord Jesus Christ,
> For the means of grace, and for the hope of
>   glory.
> And, we beseech thee,

Give us that due sense of all thy mercies,
That our hearts may be unfeignedly
    thankful;
And that we show forth thy praise,
Not only with our lips, but in our lives,
By giving up ourselves to thy service,
And by walking before thee
In holiness and righteousness all our days;
Through Jesus Christ our Lord,
To whom, with thee and the Holy Ghost,
Be all honour and glory, world without
    end. Amen.

*God, your mercy is beyond our imagining yet
our gratitude is often limited; banish from
us any indifference of spirit and fill us with
thanksgiving for your world, your people and
our salvation in Jesus Christ. Amen.*

28

Praying and Believing

W. E. Orchard

Colossians 3.12–17

For a brief period during the First World War, W. E. Orchard was one of the most famous clergymen in England. He is now almost totally forgotten. He was a minister of the Presbyterian Church of England, called to the pastorate of the King's Weigh House, Mayfair (a member church of the Congregational Union) in the summer of 1914. The King's Weigh House already possessed a tradition of liberal theology coupled with liturgical experiment, but no one foresaw how this would develop. Under Orchard's ministry the liturgy eventually grew into a high mass with traditional vestments, incense and elaborate ritual. A daily celebration of the Holy Communion was introduced. Confessions were heard. Benediction of the Blessed Sacrament drew large crowds. As many as a hundred people would take communion on weekdays. The King's Weigh House remained within the Congregational Union throughout. Years later, given my own Congregationalist background, I became fascinated with this experiment in Free Catholicism, as Orchard described it. He was also a pacifist. To preach pacifism from a pulpit in Mayfair, as well as gradually to reject all that Protestantism seemed to stand for, marked Orchard out from almost every other nonconformist minister of the period. In the early 1930s, following the death of his wife, Orchard became a Roman Catholic priest. The possibility of a Free Catholicism, untrammelled by Roman Catholic dogma but drawing on all the sacramental resources of the Catholic tradition, vanished.

William Edwin Orchard (he always preferred W. E.) had a personal conversion experience while he was still a teenager. He was 'brought into personal contact with Christ, the Saviour of the world' and felt the call to preach. His evangelical faith was a simple one, but it was to be shattered at Westminster College, Oxford, where he trained for the ordained ministry of the Presbyterian Church of England. Biblical criticism destroyed the old assurances but not the faith which underlay them. When he became the minister of St Paul's Presbyterian Church, Enfield, in 1904 he was 'anxious to clear away ... unnecessary hindrances placed in the path of those prepared to put their faith in Christ and yield themselves to His power, if only it could be shown this was a spiritual response to a spiritual appeal, and depended upon spiritual apprehension'. He believed that following Jesus consisted in practising the truths of his teaching and copying the character he displayed and that this was much more urgent than believing any doctrines about his person: 'Taking up the Cross was far more important than holding theories of the Atonement, about whose ethical soundness or intelligibility thought and enquiry was making me very suspicious'.

His church in Enfield grew quickly, and he became a close ally of R. J. Campbell, the compelling young minister of the City Temple, whose book *The New Theology*, published in 1907, created a huge national controversy. Like Orchard, Campbell argued that the moral and spiritual truths of the Christian faith were enhanced and not undermined by reinterpreting such doctrines as the virgin birth or the bodily resurrection of Christ. Both Orchard and Campbell had a deep devotion to Jesus Christ as their personal saviour, yet Campbell argued in *The New Theology* that 'Jesus was divine simply and solely because his life was never governed by any other principle. We do not need to talk of two natures in Him, or to think of the mysterious dividing line on one side of which he was human and on the other divine. In Him humanity was divinity and divinity was humanity'.

It was the furore which surrounded the publication of Campbell's book which caused Orchard to have his first doubts about his liberal theological outlook. Charles Gore wrote a thunderous response. Orchard began to be disturbed by the Hegelian premises upon which *The New Theology* was built: 'I could see that the effect of the philosophy of absolute idealism left one nothing to do but to recognise that one's own thoughts were the thoughts of the Absolute; so that Hegelianism, as had already been proved, could be just as easily a foundation for Atheism as a defence of the Christian religion'.

Campbell was seriously taken aback by Gore's response. He was at the height of his powers, with vast congregations queuing to listen to him at the City Temple. Both Orchard and Campbell came to realize that their theologies were not supporting their devotional convictions. Orchard began to realize that the fundamental weakness of his creed was its lack of a theology of the Church. Already a socialist in politics, he had remained an individualist in religion. This too became clear to Campbell. He resigned from the pastorate of the City Temple and was ordained as a priest in the Church of England. As an Anglican he exercised an unspectacular but resolutely orthodox ministry, finishing his days in the diocese of Chichester. Orchard meanwhile had begun to read the works of Catholic mystics, which deepened his appreciation of Catholic traditions of spirituality and slowly transformed the pattern of his personal devotional life.

The offer to become the minister of King's Weigh House in Mayfair came as a relief to W. E. Orchard. It had only 35 members at the time but possessed a reputation for ordered liturgical worship unusual in Congregationalism. The odd name of the church derived from a non-subscribing minister at the time of the Restoration of the monarchy in 1660 persuading some of his people to follow him out of the Church of England. He began to hold services above the King's Weigh House where foreigners' goods were weighed on import for tax purposes. It was only in the mid-nineteenth century that the church moved to Duke Street in the West End. These days the King's Weigh House has become the Ukrainian Catholic Cathedral.

Orchard quickly became a convinced pacifist and chaplain to the conscientious objectors in Wormwood Scrubs. It added to his notoriety. He was astonished to observe all Churches strangely united about the First World War. The Church seemed to have no distinctive outlook or message. He accused it of only offering a 'solemn Amen to the decisions of politicians'. He now believed the liberal understanding of the person of Jesus ministered only consolation to the soul and offered nothing about the state, war, social evils or economic problems.

He was especially hard on his fellow nonconformists, believing that their unquestioning support of the government and of the war (with the exception of the Society of Friends) meant that their claim to be 'free' churches meant nothing: 'It is no hesitant prophecy that after the War they will find that the public has discovered that their non-conformity is superficial and their freedom a shibboleth and they will be left to wilt and wither away'.

The international, indeed supra-national, character of Catholicism attracted Orchard, quite apart from the appeal of Catholic spirituality. As his pacifist preaching drew large (and sometimes critical) crowds, his Catholic practice within Congregationalism ensured his notoriety. At one level it was an astonishing success on such foreign soil. Eventually it became clear even to Orchard himself that Free

Catholicism created its own problems. Those who joined his Catholic Congregational citadel found the preaching was international and the devotion Catholic, but they had joined a communion of only one church. The individualism Orchard came to eschew was expressed in his own ministry. It led him to become a Roman Catholic where, like Campbell in the Church of England, he was faithful and orthodox but never again excited the same attention. Orchard and Campbell had lost any desire to be individualistic. Their prayers and Catholic spirituality reshaped and refashioned what they believed. At the heart of the Catholic tradition lies a willingness to give the faith of the universal church more credibility than any personal opinions or the theological fashions of the day. That does not involve the suppression of conscience, as Cardinal Newman himself indicated when asked to drink a toast to the Pope. He said he would do so, but he would drink to conscience first. Even so he knew the truth of *lex orandi, lex credenti* ('the law of praying is the law of believing'). The power of Catholic devotion and the prayer of the Church drew both Campbell and Orchard to an orthodox Christian faith. So it is no surprise that, when anyone asks Anglicans what they believe, they point first to prayer and worship. As we pray, so we believe.

Lord Jesus Christ, as we pray through you to the Father, keep us following the way which leads to the fullness of life to be found in you, the Saviour of all. Amen.

29

Faithfulness under Pressure

Joseph Hall

Mark 13.1–13

Joseph Hall was appointed as Bishop of Norwich in 1641. A Calvinist upbringing and time spent both as a student and a Fellow at Emmanuel College, Cambridge, then a centre of Puritanism, left their mark on him. Yet he was able to argue that the Roman Catholic Church was 'a visible Church' and that 'we have not detracted to hold Communion with it'. He believed that 'we have departed from the Church of Rome in those things wherein they have departed from Christ' and he certainly held no brief for Roman Catholic dogma. Even so, his words, written in 1628, were incendiary at the time. They may have been greeted by King Charles I with pleasure, married as he was to a Catholic wife, Henrietta Maria, but many others were less content. Earlier Joseph had written *Via Media, the way of peace*, attempting to find a compromise between the Calvinist and Arminian understandings of the Church and the workings of divine grace. He was looked upon with suspicion by Archbishop Laud for not being sufficiently enthusiastic in suppressing Puritan excesses. Nevertheless, the Puritans themselves looked upon him as an opponent, given his strong defence of episcopacy in the governance of the Church.

It was a moderate like Joseph Hall that the Diocese of Norwich needed in 1641. In the previous decade it had experienced one ineffective, lewd and idle bishop, then a tyrant, and finally an authoritarian bishop who quickly fell ill and died in office.

The Diocese did not see their new bishop for almost a year after his appointment. Most of that time he was imprisoned in the Tower of London, along with other bishops who had been accused of high treason by the House of Commons. The bishops had become so unpopular that protestors outside the House of Lords jostled, jeered and tried to prevent them entering the House. A number of bishops, Joseph Hall included, petitioned the King for greater security and said that until it was in place they felt obliged to absent themselves from Parliament. That meant, they believed, that any Bills passed by the House of Lords were null and void without their consideration. The public mood was not on their side, though to accuse them of high treason was extreme. Eventually they were released on a lesser charge, provided bail of £5,000 (a massive sum in those days) was paid.

So Joseph Hall eventually arrived in Norwich in the summer of 1642, a few months before the outbreak of civil war in England in which Norwich was largely on Parliament's side. By all accounts Joseph made a good impression in the Cathedral through the quality, clarity and sincerity of his preaching. However, he and his wife Elizabeth faced personal tragedy when their youngest son Edward died on Christmas Eve that year. A memorial brass to Edward Hall survives in Norwich Cathedral to this day. It describes the bishop's son, who was just 22, as 'of the most cultivated intellect and of outstanding promise. Old before his time'.

The bereaved bishop faced a fresh assault from Parliament in 1643 since he was named as one of the 'delinquents' who refused to denounce the Pope. Joseph was no Papist but defended the rights of the King and constitution of England and believed episcopacy and monarchy were both of divine origin. On 1 April 1643 Parliament issued a sequestration order against Joseph Hall depriving him of his income. Local sequestrators were appointed in Norwich with power to seize any goods as they saw fit and to make such enquiries into the recalcitrant bishop as they needed. The sequestrators came to the Bishop's Palace and seized almost everything the Halls possessed and put the goods up for public sale. As it turned out, a Mrs Goodwin, a local churchwoman whom the bishop did not know personally, put up the money to buy all the goods and promptly returned them to the bishop. The sequestrators also put the whole of the bishop's library up for sale separately. Another faithful Anglican called Mr Cook gave them enough money to secure the purchase of the books and he too promptly returned everything to the bishop.

These were to prove two heart-warming incidents in an otherwise sorry tale. In May 1643 Norwich Cathedral was despoiled. The organ was ripped out, along with altar rails, crucifixes, crosses and any depictions of saints. All these, together with copes and other vestments, were burned, much to the rejoicing of the public. Joseph Hall himself wrote of this:

> What clattering of glasses! What beating
> down of walls! What tearing up of
> monuments! What pulling down of seats!
> What wresting out of irons and brass from
> the windows and graves! What defacing of

arms! What tooting and piping upon the
destroyed organ pipes! What a hideous
triumph ... when in a kind of sacrilegious
and profane procession, all the organ pipes,
vestments, both copes and surplices ... and
the service books and singing books ... were
carried to the fire in the public marketplace;
a lewd wretch walking before the train, his
cope trailing in the dirt, with a service book
in his hand, imitating in an imperious scorn
the tune, and usurping the words of the
litany used formerly in the Church.

The Cathedral was, the bishop recorded, open on
all sides and filled with musketeers 'drinking and
tobacconing as freely as if it had turned ale house'.

Harried on all sides and deprived of his income,
Joseph was soon expelled from the Bishop's Palace
itself. He and his wife Elizabeth retreated to a house
in what was then the village of Heigham, on the
edge of the city. The house still exists. We know he
still made some appointments of clergy for parishes
and even ordained some men to the priesthood,
if surreptitiously. All Joseph had fought for as a
moderate in the Church of England seemed lost.
He continued to write, including many devotional
works, and assisted the Vicar of St Bartholomew,

Heigham. When a portion of his income was restored to him after the execution of the King, Joseph was known to visit poor widows in the parish regularly to dispense financial support and pray with them. Elizabeth died in 1652 at the age of 69, while Joseph himself lived until 1656. He preached his last sermon on his 80th birthday. We still possess a copy of it. He took for his text 1 Peter 1.17, 'And if you invoke as Father him who judges each one impartially according to his deeds, conduct yourself with fear throughout the time of your exile'.

Joseph had been in exile within his own diocese but not in exile from his Lord. Referring in the sermon to his birth, 80 years earlier, he thought that the length of his life seemed 'so short that it is gone like a tale that is told, or a dream by night, and looks but like yesterday'. He warned his congregation that they did not know the day or the hour of the ending of their own lives and needed to be good stewards of the gifts and graces God had given them. Joseph himself had certainly followed his own advice.

Lord of all ministry, we bless you for those who have borne suffering and persecution for your sake; give us a quiet spirit so that when we are disturbed by others we may hold on to you and your strengthening grace. Amen.

30

God's Heart of Love
Julian of Norwich

Colossians 1.24–29

People come from all over the world to visit St
Julian's Church, Norwich, and especially the
cell where an anchoress lived nearly 700 years ago.
We do not even know her name. We call her Julian
after the church itself, dedicated probably to Julian,
Bishop of Le Mans in the fourth century, but we are
not even certain about that. The Lady Julian had
a local reputation for holiness in her own lifetime.
The mystic Margery Kempe travelled from her home
in Bishop's Lynn (now King's Lynn) to consult
her. Margery wanted to know whether her ecstatic
experiences (which upset the clergy) were authentic
and thus of divine origin. Margery records that
Julian believed they were.

Julian had her own special experiences of God, her
'shewings'. She wrote about them very soon afterwards. Twenty years later she wrote a longer and

more considered text, the fruit of two decades of reflection and prayer. The earliest surviving book to have been written in English by a woman was focused entirely upon love, revealed to her during an illness, in which her sufferings become a window into God's nature.

Julian's writings have contemporary resonance because they are based upon intense personal experience. She lets us into the deepest and most intimate moments of her life. Julian is unsparing in her self-revelation so that we better understand the nature of the love of God. But there is not a trace of the introspection with which we are familiar in a post-Freudian world. Julian fails not only to tell us her real name but says nothing about her personal history. She shows no interest in herself at all as a subject for study. In this sense she could hardly be less contemporary. She is not the least self-absorbed. As an anchoress she had died to the world and its temptations and sought to live only for God. It is likely that Julian's vocation would have been tested by the Bishop of Norwich at the time, Henry Despenser, an authoritarian, warlike servant of King and Pope, ready to put down rebellions and raise armies. For such *shewings* of God's love to be experienced on Bishop Despenser's watch in Norwich is the sort of paradox of which God himself seems fond.

214

The most frequently quoted sentence in Julian's writings is 'all shall be well, and all shall be well, and all manner of thing shall be well'. I have heard this so inappropriately used that I once resolved never to use it again. It isn't a soothing balm suggesting that everything will turn out all right in the end, or that the disturbances in our lives are trivial. When Julian says 'all thing shall be well' it isn't to minimize suffering. Julian did not believe in short cuts in the spiritual life. She was never flaccid or comfortable. She says that it seemed to her impossible that all things should be well, but that God reminded her that what was impossible for her was not impossible for him: 'I shall preserve my word in everything, and I shall make everything well'. God does not mean that each of us in our particular circumstances will find things turn out all right so that we may know transient happiness in this life. It is an assurance that, whatever suffering comes our way, God holds us in his love and that his ultimate purposes in creation will not be defeated.

Perhaps, though, Julian's understanding of suffering is what makes her such an unlikely contemporary hero. Ours is an age which increasingly believes that 'unbearable suffering' is sufficient ground for assisted dying. In this context, Julian's own desire to suffer so that she might understand better the nature of God seems very strange. We are more likely to yearn for ways in which the path to God may be more easily accessible. By contrast, Julian made huge demands upon herself. These *shewings* of the love of God did not come by accident as surprise visitations. They were a result of her prayer and desire to be visited by 'three graces'. Opening herself to the love of God could not happen, she believed, if she did not suffer: 'I desired three graces by the gift of God. The first was to have a recollection of Christ's Passion. The second was a bodily sickness, and the third was to have, of God's gift, three wounds'.

The first of this trio of graces is familiar enough. Identifying with a biblical scene imaginatively so as to enter into its spiritual reality is a common feature of Franciscan and other spiritualities. Julian wanted to see 'with my own eyes our Lord's Passion which he suffered for me' so that she might 'suffer with him as others did who loved him'. She wanted to be alongside Mary Magdalene and the other women at the foot of the Cross.

The second grace she desired was an illness so severe that she would receive the last rites. Even though she may not die, she wanted no comfort from this life but to experience every kind of pain, bodily and spiritually, which would release her more fully into God's presence. The three wounds she sought in the third grace were the wounds of contrition, compassion and longing to be with God.

Her desire for a severe illness may seem to us masochistic or a sign of serious psychosomatic problems. Yet Julian wants simply to be purged of any self-centredness in her following of Christ. Her desire for the wound of compassion indicates how far her longing to be one with Christ in his sufferings is not for her own sake but so that she may be more open to love others, the very reason why Christ himself is willing to suffer for us. Even in her desire for an almost mortal illness, Julian says what she wants then hands her request over to God. If he doesn't will it for her 'she will not be displeased for I want nothing that you do not want'.

Julian was the contemporary of Geoffrey Chaucer, the author of *The Canterbury Tales*. She was formed within a world in which penances were offered by pilgrimages made, or money given, or acts of contrition accompanied by mortification. The physical and the spiritual worlds were wholly enmeshed. It was also a world affected by Franciscan spirituality. Francis of Assisi desired to be at one with Christ in his self-giving love. That

217

gift had been accompanied by Francis receiving the stigmata, Christ's wounds replicated on his own body. Julian makes no reference to this in her writings, but the association of bodily suffering with the opening up of the interior soul to God is central to her experience.

Many of the Lenten companions in this book have known great suffering of body, mind or spirit and sometimes all three. Most have not invited it. Few have thought it was visited upon them. But such suffering has often been a means by which God's love has been revealed in them, and not just for them but for others too. They would have been glad to have been spared it, but we and they are richer for it. During Lent and Passiontide we ponder these realities. Julian's writings, perhaps more than any other, help us glimpse why God's love is revealed in suffering humanity more vividly than in comfortable society.

> *God of compassion, take away our*
> *self-centredness and give us fresh insight into*
> *the way in which the sufferings we experience*
> *may lead us nearer your heart of love,*
> *revealed in Jesus Christ our Lord. Amen.*

31

Courage in Ministry
Susan Cole-King

2 Corinthians 5.16–21

Susan Cole-King was one of the first female Anglican priests with whom I spoke at any length. I recall our initial conversation vividly. It took place at Tymawr Convent in Wales, the home of the Society of the Sacred Cross, the community which had such a profound effect on Philip Toynbee, another companion in this book.

Susan's father was Leonard Wilson, a vicar in Durham at the time of her birth in 1934. The family moved to Hong Kong in 1938 when Leonard became Dean of the Anglican Cathedral. The outbreak of war threatened their safety and the family were evacuated to Australia. In 1941 Leonard was consecrated as Bishop of Singapore, so at the age of seven Susan was on the move again. Her sense of being an international citizen was formed while she was still young. She and her mother were sent back to

Australia shortly after the Japanese invasion of the Malay peninsula, while her father was determined to stay behind to care for his clergy and people. He was imprisoned in Changi jail and severely tortured. Eventually the family came back to England where Leonard was successively Dean of Manchester and Bishop of Birmingham. Susan enrolled as a student nurse at St Thomas' Hospital in London, and later trained as a doctor. She married Paul Cole-King, a teacher.

Two years after her qualification as a doctor in 1962, Susan and Paul moved to the newly independent Malawi, together with their young family. Hastings Banda, the new president, had established a fine reputation as a general practitioner in south London. It was hoped that he would be one of a new breed of democratic African leaders. It proved not to be the case, given the nature of the one-party state he established and its associated corruption. However, those early years were hopeful. Susan was commissioned to establish a primary health care programme across the whole country, seeking especially to ensure better health care in the rural villages. In 1973 she returned to England to a project at Sussex University focused on health care in developing countries. After her marriage came to an end she was appointed in 1980 to the staff of the World Health

Organization in Geneva. It was not congenial and a better appointment came her way a year later with UNICEF as Chief Health Adviser based in New York. Thus she settled in the United States.

Gradually she became more conscious of the spiritual dimension of healing and felt called to the priesthood. She may well have been the first English-born priest to be ordained in America. Never one to stay in one country for very long, Susan returned to England in 1988 in order to be part of the struggle towards the ordination of women in the Church of England. It was a sacrifice. She could only operate as a deacon in England, working first at Dorchester Abbey and then in charge of the parish of Drayton in the Diocese of Oxford. Male priests had to come to her parish to celebrate Holy Communion. Many people urged Susan to break ranks and not obey what they believed to be the mistaken rules of the Church of England on women ordained abroad, but she was not convinced that such actions would advance the cause responsibly. She believed in an ordered Church and gave herself to exercising a servant ministry, becoming well known as a retreat conductor and spiritual director. It was a joy to her to have her priestly vocation finally recognized in 1994 when the first women were ordained as priests in the Church of England.

At the 1998 Lambeth Conference Susan preached a memorable sermon on the Feast of the Transfiguration. She had been invited by the Primate of Japan to do so for this was also Hiroshima Day. The previous year the Anglican community in Japan, the Nippon Sei Ko Kai, had been through a lengthy process of self-examination and prayer about Japanese complicity in the Second World War and had issued a moving apology. It was a brave thing to do, far from popular in Japan. Such public repentance meant that Susan was very glad to respond.

Susan told the story of her father's torture. He was among 57 prisoners at Changi jail who were arrested by the Japanese military police in October 1943 and accused of being spies. He was tortured mercilessly. The story is well known, but Susan's words in that sermon express it vividly:

> Often he had to be carried back to his cell, almost unconscious from his wounds. On one occasion, seven men were taking it in turns to flog him and they asked him why he didn't curse them. He told them it was because he was a follower of Jesus who taught us to love one another.
> He asked himself how he could possibly love these men with their hard, cruel faces,

obviously enjoying the torture they were
inflicting. As he prayed he had a picture
of them as they might have been as little
children, and it's hard to hate little children.

... he was given a vision of those men
not as they were then, but as they were
capable of becoming, transformed by the
love of Christ.

After eight months he was released back
to Changi – one of the few who survived
the torture. For the rest of his life he
emphasised the importance of forgiveness in
his speaking and preaching.

This was no easy forgiveness, nor one that ignored
the need for repentance. Leonard Wilson refused
to succumb to the impact of the moral depravity to
which he was subjected. How he managed not to
curse his torturers, I do not know, but I recognize
that by his power to forgive he maintained his own
moral and spiritual autonomy. His soul could not
be dominated. Cruel men could have his body but
not his spirit.

In her sermon Susan said, 'Although my father was
able to forgive, and I and my family want to affirm
that unconditional forgiveness, true reconciliation
can only happen when there is an acknowledgment

223

of wrongs done, when the truth is faced and painful self-examination leads to confession and apology'.

She felt that the apology from the Japanese Church meant that the cycle of reconciliation was completed. As it was also for her father when, after the war, he returned to Singapore and confirmed one of his former torturers.

Susan finished her sermon by quoting Karl Barth reflecting on the change Christ's death on the Cross may make to any suffering person.

> Our tribulation without ceasing to be
> tribulation is transformed. We suffer as
> we suffered before, but our suffering
> is no longer a passive perplexity but is
> transformed into a pain which is creative,
> fruitful, full of power and promise. The
> road which is impassable has been made
> known to us in the crucified and the risen
> Lord.

Susan died when only 66. In her final year the Bishop of Southern Malawi, faced with the escalation of Aids in his country, had asked her to return and help 'find the link between Aids and spirituality'. She spent four months in Malawi enabling clergy, teachers, parents and sufferers to talk about what was often an unspoken subject, too horrific to contemplate. Her medical, priestly and pastoral skills were well used, and in a country where there were no female Anglican clergy. Some breakthroughs in understanding were achieved. At the time of her death, Susan was planning to return.

Susan lived an exceptionally full life of service and devotion. Like many people, she came to appreciate and understand her father, even to love him more deeply, in the final years of her own life. Sometimes we need a lifetime's experience to understand the gift of remarkable parents.

Christ our servant, may we follow you in using our gifts fully in your service and, when our courage to forgive is tested, may our will be strengthened by your unchanging love for us. Amen.

32

Broken for Christ

Bernard Walke

2 Corinthians 1.8–14

On St Matthew's Day 1998 I was at St Hilary in west Cornwall to dedicate an icon in memory of a faithful parishioner and to rededicate some refurbished items which dated back to the incumbency of Bernard Walke. That evening we felt as if we were doing just a little more to restore St Hilary's beauty after the destruction visited on the church on 8 August 1932 when a group of extreme Protestant iconoclasts smashed images, damaged and removed paintings and destroyed tabernacles and much church furniture. They did allow the vicar to remove the Blessed Sacrament from the church but Bernard Walke never removed from his mind the images of the scenes he witnessed that day. The sight of men standing on the altar hacking away at the reredos or smashing an image of Our Lady haunted him.

The excuse for this desecration was that Bernard Walke had ignored the direction of the Truro Consistory Court to remove the tabernacle from the high altar and make some other changes to the interior of his church. Walke did not recognize the authority of the Chancellor or his court over such matters, so refused to cooperate. This was on the grounds that it was not a spiritual court because 'its spiritual nature was lost on the day it allowed an appeal to the secular court on matters spiritual'. Walke's attitude was common enough among Anglo-Catholic clergy who had suffered disruption and persecution from Protestant agitators, especially after the passage of the Public Worship Regulation Act in 1874. St Hilary was singled out for attention since the whole of Britain knew of the village because some of the first live outside broadcasts ever made on BBC Radio were of Bernard Walke's Christmas plays.

Bernard Walke was born in 1874, the son of a priest in Wiltshire. He was ordained to a curacy at St Ives and then moved to Cornwall's south coast as curate at Polruan, a fishing village of narrow streets, where a daughter church dedicated to St Saviour had been built within the parish of Lanteglos-by-Fowey. A degree of eccentricity was noticeable about him even then. His cat came to church with him every day and took to ascending the pulpit and sitting on the ledge while Bernard preached, once jumping into the lap of an elderly lady in the front pew. When his vicar resigned in 1912 he had to leave. There was no security of tenure for curates. The Bishop of Truro suggested unhelpfully that good priests were wanted in the north of England (they still are) but by then Bernard had married the artist Anne Fearon who was already part of the Cornish artistic community. An offer out of the blue from a private patron to be the next incumbent of St Hilary was accepted by telegram immediately without Bernard and Annie (as he always called her) knowing anything about this small village. They were not impressed on first arrival. However, Bernard's book *Twenty Years at St Hilary,* written from his bed in Tehidy's sanatorium near Camborne while he recovered from tuberculosis, gives an evocative and detailed account of the remarkable things that happened there in the interwar years.

The people of the parish could not fail to notice a radical change in the worship of their church from the first Sunday Bernard Walke officiated. The Reformation was abolished. The mass was reintroduced (in Latin, too, for the most part) and to prepare for it he had trained a local boy as a thurifer and another to make the responses. Few were converted to the Catholic faith in those early days but they did respond to their new vicar's preaching at the evening service. 'A proper preacher' was how they described him. Gradually, as they got to know their unusual parson and his artistic wife, affection grew between them. As Walke himself put it, his people initially 'didn't altogether hold with his goings on' but thought 'the parson isn't a bad old sort'.

That feeling grew when local people recognized that their parson and his wife loved not only the church but all sorts and conditions of people as well. In time, an old pub, *The Jolly Tinners*, was taken over to accommodate ten destitute children, five boys and five girls. They were given a home under a benevolent matron. The name of the defunct pub was a reminder of better times in Cornwall when tin mining was prosperous. Walke worked hard to help substantial numbers of unemployed Cornish miners find work. Together with others, and with some support from the wider Church community in Cornwall including his bishop, plans were hatched to reopen a disused mine to provide fresh employment. The project was not finally realized because of failure to find the full capital needed but Father Bernard Walke's name was one which many Cornish miners, mostly Methodists themselves, treasured.

In 1917, Bernard and Annie Walke both joined the Fellowship of Reconciliation, a Christian pacifist organization dedicated to bringing an end to the First World War. They went to many peace meetings, sharing platforms with Quakers, one of the signs of the surprising ecumenism of this otherwise resolutely uncompromising Anglo-Catholic priest. Many of the leading artists and writers of the day came to St Hilary. Compton MacKenzie and Walter de la Mare were among Bernard and Annie's friends. Ernest and Dod Proctor, Roger Fry and the child prodigy Joan Manning-Sanders, who painted panels in the Lady Chapel when just 12 years old, all contributed artworks. The church became a riot of colour and beauty. It was the centre of community life as well. A Christmas play, *Bethlehem*, which Bernard wrote, featuring people of all ages from the parish as the actors, drew crowds. The idea owed much to the mediaeval mystery play tradition. A chance meeting led to interest from the BBC and in the early days of radio the St Hilary Christmas play gained huge popularity. The actors' Cornish accents added to the sense that these were rural people in a faraway land telling a story locked in time but for all time. After the first broadcast, Bernard received a letter from

231

Sir John Reith telling him that he had been listening with the Prime Minister, Ramsay Macdonald, and that they wished to thank him for such a beautiful production of the Nativity. St Hilary blazed a trail for the later plays of Dorothy L. Sayers on radio mentioned elsewhere in this book.

Bernard Walke thought that what he created at St Hilary could have been replicated all over England, returning the Church of England to the Catholic faith and capturing the involvement of the whole community in its sacramental life. Even before the physical destruction of his church in 1932 he began to see that England was becoming more secular rather than more Christian. Nor was Anglo-Catholicism developing in the way he hoped. His tendency to be dispirited was exacerbated by the destruction of his church and was quickly followed by the breakdown of his health. He and his wife retired to Mevagissey where he died in 1941. His heart was broken.

This story of an imaginative and courageous pastoral ministry does not have a happy ending. For years afterwards, a sadness hung over St Hilary. *Twenty Years at St Hilary* is a book written by a beaten man, who followed the way of the Cross in a manner he never expected. But brokenness – of hearts as well as bodies – may be the price of following Christ.

*Lord Jesus Christ, your body was broken on
the Cross through the sin of the world, take
our brokenness in body, mind or spirit and
mend us with the instruments of your Passion.
Amen.*

33

Learning to Die Well

Philip Toynbee

Romans 14.7–12

Hidden away in the Welsh countryside, just a few miles from Monmouth, is a small community of Anglican contemplative nuns, the Society of the Sacred Cross. Founded originally in Chichester, they moved to their present home, Tymawr Convent, in 1923. I have known them for over 40 years, the consequence of a contemporary of mine at the University of Lancaster in the days of student protest doing something as unlikely as becoming an Anglican contemplative nun. Alongside worship and prayer, the nuns kept cows and chickens for many years, seeking to live as much as they could from their land.

In the mid-1970s another self-supporting farming community established itself a few miles from them. Among these new arrivals in Wales was Philip Toynbee, the writer and literary reviewer for *The*

Observer. He belonged more naturally to urban bohemian life than the routines of rural agriculture. Ideas were the driving force in Philip's life. This move to Wales, along with a mixed group of supporters, was the product of a growing ecological awareness. It was more ideological than practical.

Philip quickly came to know the Society of the Sacred Cross with their longer experience in farming a few acres successfully. Soon, Philip and his wife Sally moved into their own house and their new community became more of a commune. The unexpected consequence of all this was Philip's deep and growing attachment to the Sisters at Tymawr. I first met Philip on one of my visits. He was a very unlikely convert to any sort of orthodox Christianity. That he should have felt so much at home in that religious community was a sign of how inclusive and attractive the religious life can be.

Philip's father was the eminent historian Arnold Toynbee. His maternal grandfather was the classicist Gilbert Murray. Philip's early life was shaped by books, ideas and words. His own novels never matched in quality the creative instincts which lay within him. For decades he worked on a novel in verse, *Pantaloon*, which would have been an epic in several volumes, few of which ever saw publication.

What did emerge was largely greeted with mystifi-
cation. Philip was a brilliant critic and reviewer of all
sorts of literary genres. It was almost as if his own
powers of criticism were so keen they either inhibited
his creative impulse or caused him to overelaborate.
Yet two books were produced towards the end of
his life which were well received, but not written as
books at all. *Part of a Journey* and *End of a Journey*
contained extracts from his personal journals during
his final years before he died of cancer in June 1981.
Philip Toynbee did find a community in Wales – but
it was not the sort he expected to discover. It was
one focused on the life, death and resurrection of
Jesus Christ. While Philip was never likely to submit
to the authority of a fallible Church, he became a
praying and questioning follower of Jesus Christ. It
distressed him that Sally didn't travel with him on
this spiritual journey. He also had a very puzzled
family since the journalist Polly Toynbee is his
daughter from his first marriage.

In 1979, Philip was invited to give the Essex Hall
Lecture for the General Assembly of Unitarian and
Free Christian Churches. Within this lecture he
described why he called himself a Christian:

> I call myself a Christian because I discern in
> the New Testament a man whose life, death

and central teaching penetrate more deeply into the mysterious reality of our condition than anyone or anything else has ever done. In the Gospels, the Acts and Epistles I find a total view of what man is, of what he could and ought to be, which evokes a response in me such as no other writings have ever evoked. For me the heart of the New Testament is the assurance that there is a God whose power lies in his total love; that this God not only transcends the natural world but also enters that world through the minds and hearts of men. I accept, with grateful love, the supreme commandment given to his disciples by the Jesus of St. Luke's gospel: 'Thou shalt love the Lord thy God with all thy heart, and with all thy soul, and with all thy strength, and with all thy mind; and thy neighbour as thyself'.

I believe that man's highest destiny on earth is to be born again into the Kingdom of Heaven. I believe that God is spirit, and that those who would come to him must come in spirit and in truth ... I know that for me Jesus is the Way, the Truth and the Life and this way is my only hope of learning to love God as I am already loved by him.

End of a Journey was published after Philip's death. In it he struggles with the meaning of suffering and death. In the last month of his life he had a final operation and wondered whether he would die under the anaesthetic. He feared this possibility: 'There would be no dying, and if I don't have to face an utterly reducing process of dehumanization I do not want to be deprived of the proper stages [of dying]. I want to learn all I can from it ...'

Philip Toynbee's belief that he could learn from his dying wasn't just the consequence of a curious mind. It was a statement of faith in a life beyond this one, however mysterious and obscure. He doesn't expand on what he means by 'the proper stages of dying', but whatever view we may take of assisted dying, much of the debate fails to credit the experience of dying with any positive character at all. Philip Toynbee did not want his death to be preceded by a peaceful oblivion. Through the Society of the Sacred Cross he discovered that concentration upon the death of Jesus Christ does not feed morbidity but results in a joyful self-giving love. Philip wrote, 'I believe that Jesus died for us in the sense that he accepted an agonizing death rather than abjure his message of a heavenly love which far transcends even the most venerable of holy laws and sacred traditions'.

239

Philip often concluded his formal prayers 'through Jesus Christ our brother and bringer of light'. That light shone through the Cross and carried Philip towards a greater light which drew him on. Since his death, accounts of Philip's life sometimes refer to these final years as 'vaguely Christian'. There never seemed anything vague in Philip. His testimony to Jesus Christ remains powerful, couched as it was in the language of the Authorized Version of the Bible which he loved so much.

> *God of compassion, in life and in death we*
> *rely on your mercy; help us to discover Jesus*
> *Christ as our constant and utterly reliable*
> *companion, our brother and bringer of light.*
> *Amen.*

34

Weeping over the Holy City

John Aves

Luke 19.41–44

John Aves was one of those priests whom bishops treasure. Loved by the people of his parishes, he had an infectious joy about him which made the Christian faith attractive. He also possessed immense curiosity. He wanted to know how other people lived. That's what led him to spend the last three months of his life in the Holy Land. Not that anyone knew it would be the last three months. He went there as part of the Ecumenical Accompaniment Programme in Palestine and Israel (EAPPI). But, good though the programme was, John felt he wasn't getting close enough to the Palestinian people. So he went to live alongside them in the Dheisheh refugee camp near Bethlehem. It was in Bethlehem where he died suddenly in 2004, aged just 52, only a short time before he was due back home.

There is now a well-established educational project in John's honour, providing bursaries and other support for students from the refugee camps to study at Bethlehem University. Despite such a brief stay a decade ago, John is still remembered at Dheisheh. His life there may have been short but it had an incarnational quality. John always identified with the people he served in his ministry.

John came from a farming family on the Suffolk–Norfolk border. His faith came alive in the context of an ordinary country parish. He never dismissed the value of tiny, elderly, rural congregations. Seventeen fruitful years as Rector of Attleborough and Besthorpe in south-west Norfolk were followed by John's appointment as Priest in Charge of St Giles, Norwich and Continuing Ministerial Development Adviser in the diocese. Early in my time as Bishop of Norwich I realized that he was one of those clergy who believed he had a pastoral ministry to his bishop as well as his bishop having a pastoral ministry to him. It was the best sort of continuing ministerial development I could receive.

A bishop's life has many dangers and temptations. Perhaps the most spiritually hazardous is to cease to be on the receiving end of pastoral ministry at all. It affects all clergy, of course, but I understand why so many priests feel inhibited from offering the bishop any pastoral care. It's why bishops often find chaplains so necessary. A bishop who is always in the mode of transmission, whether as preacher or pastor, will soon become empty within. That's why I've always been grateful for just a few priests in my care, John among them, whose words of pastoral wisdom, gentle enquiries and occasional admonitions over a shared whisky have been balm to the soul. I'm always conscious of what I owe John when I'm with his widow Anne and his adult children Ben and Ed, who are all committed to continuing the work in the Palestinian Territories their husband and father started. As an example of how to grieve creatively it has been a remarkable witness. As it was, I knew we would have a major Holy Land project in the Diocese on John's return. I'd been getting emails from him preparing me. Little did I realize that it would turn out to be in his memory.

When Jesus washes the feet of his disciples we readily understand why they thought it strange that their Lord and Master should offer this basic service. Their protest was natural. But I've always found the most striking foot washing in the gospels to be the one where the woman of bad reputation washes Jesus' feet with her tears and dries them with her hair. It's not only the sensuality of the episode which

243

makes it genuinely shocking but also the way in which Jesus allows himself to be ministered to. The care of another human being for us enhances the fullness of our own humanity. Jesus, fully human, responds with affection, appreciation and gratitude to the ministrations of this unidentified woman. It's not only bishops who should follow Christ's example and take such risks. Social convention aside, such things are no risk at all. We all need to receive ministry and be indebted to the spontaneous care of those for whom we also care. John knew all this but rediscovered it vividly in Bethlehem.

The Shepherds' Fields at Beit Sahour, a short distance from Bethlehem, is the traditional site for the angels' announcement of the birth of Christ. The setting is a peaceful one, disturbed only by the arrival of regular pilgrimage groups. There's always space to sit quietly. In autumn 2013 I gazed across the valley from the Shepherds' Fields to an Israeli settlement on the opposite hill. The Israeli security fence separated the two, rendering what was once fertile land increasingly barren. Two thousand years after the proclamation of the birth of the Prince of Peace, division, enmity and suspicion seemed as embedded as ever. Jesus wept over Jerusalem. It is hard not to shed tears today as one sees a wall of division ever more securely constructed.

At the Shepherds' Fields I remembered John Aves. Just the day before he died he sent an email home which said:

> Do I come back from the Holy Land
> with much hope? The answer is yes. Why?
> Because I see the story of Christ here, not
> only in the holy places and the Bible but
> in the countless stories of courage and
> dignity I have witnessed. I see tremendous
> God-given hope in the centre where I've
> worked. It is run by Palestinians who
> are placing their hope in educating their
> children, giving them self-confidence and
> language and computer skills to carry on the
> long-term struggle with dignity and grace.

Bethlehem University is a beacon of hope in the Palestinian Territories. So many young Palestinians there, forbidden to go to Jerusalem and Israel, do travel widely in their minds. They believe in education and hope for a better future. They do not despair. The vast majority seek peace with all their brothers and sisters. The message proclaimed in the Shepherds' Fields two millennia ago is as fresh as ever.

Prince of peace, you wept over Jerusalem;
prevent our tears over injustice rendering us

*helpless but give us determination to act in
solidarity with the despised and the afflicted
wherever they are found. Amen.*

35

Unjust Suffering

Hugo Gryn

1 Peter 3.13–17

In the 1980s there was no specialist on interfaith matters on the Archbishop of Canterbury's staff so the Archbishop's Chaplain then had this area of work included as part of his brief. Within 12 months of my arrival to work for Robert Runcie a fatwa had been imposed by the Ayatollah Khomeini on Salman Rushdie following the publication of *The Satanic Verses*. That drove inter-faith issues rapidly up the agenda.

Salman Rushdie's books were burned by a radicalized Islamic community, the size of which had grown, rather unnoticed by the country at large. Only the Archbishop of Canterbury appeared to be able to convene national meetings of Muslim community leaders. Government ministers and politicians then barely knew who they were, and were largely untrusted by them. But local bishops such as the

Bishop of Bradford, Roy Williamson, had fostered trusting relationships. The Church of England was doing its work for the whole community as it experienced radical religious reshaping. Nowadays things are totally different. A quarter of a century ago I was not alone in being on a huge learning curve about other world faiths.

The one world faith other than Christianity I thought I knew something about was Judaism. (As it happens I was wrong.) In London the first rabbi I came to know well was Hugo Gryn. He was already a familiar voice on radio as the most perceptive yet emollient member of the panel on Radio 4's *The Moral Maze*. I held him in awe. He presided over one of the largest synagogues in Western Europe with around 3,000 families attached to it. He found time to educate me about reformed Judaism. In that first year of my work at Lambeth, the UK Interfaith Network was formed, the brainchild of a percipient ex-civil servant called Brian Pearce. Hugo was one of its first joint chairs. When I was consecrated as a bishop in 1993 in Westminster Abbey he was among the Jews in the congregation there to support me. His ecumenical spirit was astonishing. Little did we know he was then entering his final years. Cancer was diagnosed in 1996 and Hugo died within a few weeks. Michael Buerk, the chair of *The Moral Maze*, was also a newsreader at the time. He announced Hugo's death to the television audience with tears in his eyes.

Hugo was born into a relatively prosperous Jewish family in Berehovo in 1930. He used to tell a story about a man from Berehovo who arrived at the gates of heaven. Before he was to be allowed in he had to tell the story of his life. The man began, 'I was born in the Austro-Hungarian Empire to God fearing parents, received my education in Czechoslovakia and started work as an apprentice in Hungary. For a time I also worked in Germany, but I raised my family and did most of my life's work in the Soviet Union'. The gatekeeper in heaven was impressed. 'You certainly travelled and moved about a great deal'. 'No,' the man protested, 'I never left Berehovo!'

Berehovo lies in the foothills of the Carpathian mountain range. It wasn't a good place for Jews to be towards the end of the Second World War. Hugo was among 10,000 Jews confined to the Berehovo ghetto in April 1944. Within a month he was sent to Auschwitz. He looked older than his 14 years and was told to say that he was a carpenter and joiner. He and his father were identified as workers. His grandfather and his ten-year-old brother went immediately to the gas chambers.

Hugo and his father somehow survived two death marches to other camps and perhaps it was only his youth which enabled him to survive a terrible year until liberation at the end of the war. Tragically his father died in May 1945, broken by the experience.

A few months later Hugo came to Great Britain where he continued his studies. He discovered Progressive Judaism and was guided towards the rabbinate. After further studies in the United States he was ordained and served in Bombay, New York, Prague and Budapest before becoming an associate rabbi at the West London Synagogue in 1964. He served there, in time as its senior rabbi, until his death.

When I first came to know Hugo Gryn it intrigued me that someone who had been treated with such cruelty by his fellow human beings possessed such reservoirs of human sympathy. He seemed able to embrace a huge range of convictions, both religious and secular. For the first two or three decades after the war he spoke little about his teenage experience of the death camps. Things began to change in the last decade or so of Hugo's life. Holocaust deniers seemed to be gaining a hearing. For a whole year Hugo's public speaking engagements were entirely related to themes from the Holocaust.

With his daughter Naomi he made a memorable television programme for Channel 4, returning to Berehovo where he relived his childhood experiences, including his incarceration. It was repeated after his death and remains a moving testimony.

When Hugo was a slave labourer in the Lieberose Camp, he worked from dawn to dusk six and a half days a week, whatever the weather, and with little nourishment. Only on Sunday afternoons were there a few hours of rest. One Sunday afternoon everyone was surprised to be told that, courtesy of the Red Cross, all prisoners would be allowed to send a postcard anywhere in the world. People were excited, including Hugo. He got his postcard and sat down to write. Gradually he realized there was no one to whom he could write a postcard. No one in the world knew or cared whether he would live or die. (As it turned out, his mother survived the war, though at the time Hugo thought only he and his father were left.) Hugo realized he was totally alone. A few weeks later on the Day of Atonement he spent his time crying, feeling abandoned. He spoke of gaining a curious inner peace for he felt God was crying too: "And I understood a bit of the revelation that is implicit in Auschwitz. It is about man and his idols. God, the God of Abraham, could not abandon me, only I could abandon God."

Hugo spoke of creation as an ongoing process and believed that revelation was ongoing too. In his imprisonment, despite the cruelty and heartlessness, he gained a fresh understanding of God. There was a revelation at Auschwitz but he spoke of it as one 'of a dreadful and devastating sort'. Evil was harnessed to up-to-date technology within an atmosphere denuded of morality. The murder of innocent men, women and children was 'scientific'. Murder was made a virtue and the death of innocents a cause for celebration.

Hugo was never sure that time was a great healer. But he did believe it gave him a perspective. Thinking back, he realized that he had never been into any of Berehovo's three big and beautiful churches. He realized that probably none of Berehovo's Christians had been in any of the Jewish synagogues. That was one of the spurs to Hugo working for good inter-faith dialogue. He saw the consequences of living in spiritual silos. He was eventually brought out of his own silo on the Day of Atonement when he cried bitterly and believed that God was crying with him. His understanding of God changed when he realized that God himself could be violated. Hugo used to say the important question was not 'Where was God at Auschwitz?' The real question was 'Where was man at Auschwitz?'

God of suffering humanity, look with pity
on those who suffer cruelty; convict those who
enslave and maltreat their neighbours; and
assist us to understand that you share our
tears and suffer with us, longing that we may
know your presence in our distress. Amen.

36

Patriot of God's Kingdom

Edith Cavell

Matthew 16.24–28

Edith Cavell's death before a German firing squad in occupied Belgium in 1915 may have had very few observers, but news spread rapidly. Edith was a British nurse in her 50th year. The German decision to execute her for treason was presented as barbaric. It provided the Allies with a major propaganda weapon. Her name was invoked in the recruitment of young soldiers. She would have not sought such fame. There was nothing showy or conceited about her. The way she met her death was very much in keeping with the way she lived her life.

Edith was born in 1865, the eldest of four children of the Reverend Frederick Cavell and his wife Louisa. Her father was vicar of Swardeston, a village about four miles from Norwich. He served there for 45 years and seems to have been very much a clergyman of his time – dutiful and devout but perhaps rather dull. Edith didn't relish his sermons. But she did catch the faith and possessed a strong sense of service.

Edith was largely educated at home by her father and a governess. Only in later adolescence did she receive any formal education. She then became a governess in another rural vicarage but her mind and spirit, while never rebellious, were too large for such a restricted world. Still in her adolescence she wrote to a cousin, 'Someday, somehow, I am going to do something useful. I don't know what it will be. I only know that it will be something for people. They are, most of them, so helpless, so hurt and so unhappy'.

Edith's parents possessed some sense of adventure, otherwise they would not have taken the family on a visit to Germany in 1888. This kindled Edith's desire to live and work abroad. She got her wish two years later when she became a governess for the children of a lawyer in Brussels. Her five years with the François family were happy enough but it was not to be her life's work. That would only begin once she applied for training as a nurse. By then she was already 30. It was a profession which, thanks to Florence Nightingale, had grown in esteem.

Advances in medical science and the opening of new hospitals meant that there were opportunities even for a late entrant like Edith. Her Brussels connection meant that once trained she was quickly recruited as a nurse in Belgium. Dr Antoine Depage wanted Edith to pioneer the training of nurses there. The L'école Belge d'Infirmières Diplômées was opened in 1907. Edith excelled in this work. Within five years the school was providing nurses for three hospitals, 24 community schools and 13 kindergartens. At the outbreak of the First World War the school and its clinic became a Red Cross hospital. Since Belgium was quickly overrun by the German forces, British soldiers were left stranded. Some found their way to Edith's training school. She tended them and helped them make their escape to neutral territory in the Netherlands. Up to 200 British, French and Belgian soldiers gained freedom that way. It was a violation of both German law and the First Geneva Convention. Edith knew that, but believed it was humanitarian work. She would care equally for injured German soldiers or anyone sick or in need.

Edith was arrested in August 1915, the consequence of her treatment of a Belgian collaborator whom she had helped. Edith freely confessed what she had done, believing it to be morally right even if contrary to German law in an occupied country. (The Germans seem not to have mentioned the First Geneva Convention.) The sentence had to be death by firing squad. They seemed to have no choice.

There was tragedy in Edith's final hours. There wasn't much time between the sentence being given one afternoon and her execution the following morning. Even so, the lethargy and self-absorption of officials who should have appealed for clemency on her behalf is a striking feature of the details of the story. It need not have been like this. Yet Edith did not complain.

Her body was returned to England after the end of the First World War. It is not easy to recapture the enormous scale of the progress of her coffin in May 1919 from Brussels to London with crowds and services everywhere, including Westminster Abbey. Brought by special train to Norwich she was buried in an area immediately south of the Cathedral appropriately called Life's Green.

Her memorial carries the inscription 'nurse, patriot and martyr'. No one can doubt she was a nurse, who found the vocation for which she yearned in her adolescence. She was certainly a *patriot*. She declared that she was happy to die for her country but she did not want to be seen as a war hero:

'Think of me only as a nurse who tried to do her duty'. Her loyalty to her native land was strong. Even so, she said, 'Patriotism is not enough. I must have no hatred or bitterness towards anyone'. She had a greater loyalty to all humanity. To be a patriot of the kingdom of God was what truly mattered. *Martyr?* It is well known that the word *martyr* means 'witness'. Edith Cavell witnessed to her faith by the manner she prepared for her death.

She asked for a book during that time. *The Imitation of Christ* by Thomas à Kempis. It wasn't exactly routine reading in an English country vicarage in the late nineteenth century so it may say a lot about Edith. She marked a good many sentences in her copy while she awaited her sentence and execution. These are just three of them:

> Vanity it is, to wish to live long, and to be careless to live well.

> Occasions of adversity best discover how great virtue or strength each one has. Such occasions do not make a man frail, but they show what he is.

> If Jesus be with thee no enemy shall be able to hurt thee.

259

Edith seems to have thought of herself as the ordinary product of ordinary Christianity, as practised in an ordinary country vicarage. It shows how powerful the ordinary can be.

> *God of peace, keep our eyes fixed on you*
> *whenever conflict surrounds us, and give*
> *us strength to witness to your saving love*
> *that we may be true patriots of your coming*
> *Kingdom. Amen.*

37

God's Exhausting Love

W. H. Vanstone

Luke 23.32–46

Just before my 28th birthday in 1979 I was licensed as priest-in-charge of Christ the King, Haldens, in Welwyn Garden City. It was part of a large parish which became a team ministry, in which I would serve as a team vicar. The church had been built in 1965 on a council estate of around 6,000 people. I was the seventh priest to be given responsibility for this church in its short life. It was a modest building, not very fetching from the outside. A visiting preacher once drove past thinking it was a fire station. But it was attractive within, built with a stone altar set into the east wall with six large candles placed firmly upon it, the consequence of a fruitless attempt to withstand liturgical revision. By the time I arrived, a table stood in the spacious sanctuary. The worship was modern Catholic.

The congregation grew but there were times of

disappointment. Some of the new Christians in whom I had invested a great deal of time lapsed quickly. Keen confirmation candidates who came to the Eucharist two or three times a week sometimes declared themselves unbelievers within a couple of years. It all felt very fragile even when numbers were good. I couldn't help wondering whether most of the seed was sown in rather thin soil where thistles and weeds grow easily and choke the new Christian disciple.

A couple of years into my ministry there I read W. H. Vanstone's *Love's Endeavour, Love's Expense*. It transformed my ministry. I saw the value of all we did in church in a new way. I began to regard my own ministry as one which didn't depend upon the worth other people on the estate gave it. I was already aware that the vast majority of the population were not really bothered whether a priest was there or not.

What drew me to Vanstone's book was its deceptive autobiographical introduction. He said very little about himself (I came to know him later and realized how spare he could be) but a great deal about a new church on a council estate he had been asked by his bishop to lead 20 years previously. He was the first priest of this new church, planned before the estate was constructed. The church would be built alongside the houses as the people moved in.

He described his visits to the estate in the weeks before he moved there. He was taken aback by the way in which no one he met showed the slightest interest in the church. He became downhearted but then realized this prevailing attitude made the church even more important and not less. The church on that estate would be the place where the love of God would receive an explicit response where he was generally otherwise unacknowledged. God's love was not absent from the lives of those uninvolved in the life of the Church. It was more often tragically ignored than explicitly rejected. Responding to God's costly love for everyone: that was what the Church was for. Reading Vanstone's book made me the more convinced that our weekday Eucharists with tiny congregations were deeply worthwhile. The way we offered our worship mattered. It fed our service of the community around. I became the first chair of a Residents Association set up in the parish – but it wasn't a search for a relevant role which caused me to do so. It flowed from our response to the love of God.

Vanstone's book made a deep impact on my ministry since I realized that his theology was honed on the anvil of pastoral experience on another modern council estate. He had waited more than 20 years to write his first book, despite having been one of the most brilliant scholars at Cambridge in his generation. He had studied with Paul Tillich in the United States. As a very young man he was a tutor at Westcott House in Cambridge, with Robert Runcie among his students. He was set for a glittering career as an academic theologian. Instead, he became a parish priest in a very unglamorous parish. I loved him for that alone, but it was what he had written which mattered too.

Love is a rather overworked word in the Christian vocabulary. It was a commonplace word in the popular music of the 1960s. The Beatles sang 'All you need is love' and thought themselves profound. Trendy vicars put flowers in their hair. Love, freed from all constraint and restraint, was thought to bring peace and harmony to the world. Love was at the heart of protest as well as passion.

I was too much one of my generation to be unaffected by the spirit of the age. 'All you need is love' wasn't something to argue against, yet instinctively I believed there was more to be said than was to be found in that repetitive song. 'God so loved the world that he gave his only Son so that everyone who believes in him should not perish but have eternal life' (John 3.16).

There was nothing sentimental about Bill Vanstone's understanding of love. I call him Bill but I would never have dared do so when I knew him. He was always 'Canon Vanstone' to me and I was always 'Mr James' to him. Our contact began when I worked for Robert Runcie at Lambeth Palace. Bill Vanstone was a reliable source of an original thought for a sermon or an address. He would often see things distinctively.

Bill Vanstone's understanding of God's love was inseparable from the Passion and death of Christ. God's offering of himself was total and costly. Nothing was held back. I recall him telling a story about a surgeon called to operate on a young man of great promise who had had an accident and for whom no other remedy was possible. The surgeon had never performed this operation before. It took seven hours of intense concentration in which a single small error would have led to the young man's death. In the event the operation was a triumph. But after it was over a nurse had to lead the surgeon from the operating theatre like a blind man since he had become so utterly exhausted and spent. Vanstone comments that 'such is the likeness of God, wholly given, spent and drained in that sublime self-giving which is the ground and source and origin of the universe'.

W. H. Vanstone's three books contain scarcely any footnotes or references to other publications. He was a thinker, reflecting on pastoral experience, the scriptures and the sacraments and needing little else, apart from cigarettes. I was surprised to discover he was dependent on tobacco since I had thought him an ascetic dependent on God alone. In truth it was a reminder of his humanity. He was eventually persuaded to become a residentiary canon at Chester Cathedral, though his heart never left his council estate. He had more time for wayward boys from poor homes than he did for the university world in which he shone or the world of bishops and so-called senior clergy. He knew where he was called. Long-suffering pastoral ministry was to him properly reflective of a loving, patient God, exhausting himself for his creation.

> *Self-giving Lord, you spent yourself on the Cross and held nothing back from us; may we be unsparing in our service in response to your costly love for us. Amen.*

38

Priestly Sacrifice
Michael Evans

Hebrews 5.5–10

In January 2011, Michael Evans, the Roman Catholic Bishop of East Anglia, wrote to the people of his diocese to tell them he would die soon. He was just 59. The news was not unexpected. Six years previously he'd been diagnosed with an aggressive form of prostate cancer. He had decided to be open about what was happening to him. For some time it did not seem to make much difference to his ministry, except that he seemed to work even harder. Faith and willpower were as important as his treatment in keeping him going. Now the doctors gave him a matter of weeks to live. 'As I live now under the shadow of death, my prayer is very much that of St Paul that I may know something of the power of Christ's Resurrection and a share in his sufferings, trusting that the Lord is with me. I pray that even now I can joyfully witness something of the good news we are all called to proclaim'.

He thanked his people for the enormous amount of love and support he had received and asked them simply to pray for him as the best thing they could now do. Rather to everyone's surprise, and also his own, Michael lived for another six months. In July 2011, St John's Cathedral in Norwich saw one of its largest ever congregations for Michael's requiem mass. The third Roman Catholic Bishop of East Anglia had ministered to his geographically widespread diocese for just eight years. They were memorable, not only for the Roman Catholic community, but for many others like myself who grieved the loss of a friend, colleague and partner in the Gospel.

Michael was one of those priests who was genuinely surprised and humbled to become a bishop. He didn't fake his sense of unworthiness and never became in the least prelatical. Those who knew him best were relieved that someone with so quick a theological mind and also so fully shaped and formed by the Second Vatican Council had been included in the Catholic hierarchy. Michael's ideal Pope was Paul VI, a relatively unfashionable figure. Any supporter of Leeds United who also loved Shostakovich (Michael was passionate about both) knew how to cope with the unfashionable. He served most of his episcopate during the papacy of Benedict XVI, though there was a good deal of Pope Francis in Michael, given his desire for simplicity – in liturgy as well as in habits of life. He was loyal but some of the initiatives coming from Rome (which he had never visited until he became a bishop) did not work with the grain of his ministry. I believe he had never presided at a Tridentine Mass, nor possessed any desire to do so. Nor did he think Pope Benedict's longing to reintegrate the Society of Pius X (the breakaway group of traditional Catholics) would end in anything other than tears. He was right. He was still well enough to take part in the visit of Pope Benedict to Britain in September 2010, though the introduction a few months later of the Ordinariate (intended for Anglicans to become part of the Roman Catholic Church and retain their own 'patrimony') struck him as muddle-headed, the consequence of too few people in Rome understanding Anglicanism at all.

Michael had committed himself for a good many years to another cause that, if not unfashionable, scarcely hit the headlines – the promotion of Roman Catholic-Methodist relations. In 1996 he became part of the International Joint Council for Dialogue between Catholicism and World Methodism. In Norwich he and I led regular joint teaching sessions in each other's cathedrals – on baptism, social justice, prayer and worship, and once on the Anglican-Roman Catholic report on *Mary: Grace and Hope in Christ*. Some of the Catholic faithful remarked on these occasions that we seemed to have difficulty in finding things to disagree about. That was largely the point.

Michael had a strong sense of social justice. He had been a member of Amnesty International for 30 years before his resignation in 2007. He felt provoked to do so when Amnesty included a woman's right to choose to end her pregnancy on a list of essential human rights. Previously Amnesty had maintained a neutral line on abortion. Many who did not endorse all Catholic teaching on abortion were grateful to Michael for making Amnesty think again about how its own policies could affect the conscience of its members.

A south Londoner by origin, Michael went straight to seminary from school. In time he taught at St John's Seminary at Wonersh in Surrey before becoming the parish priest of St Augustine's, Tunbridge Wells. It was a thriving parish. While he was there and throughout his life he was a regular visitor to Taizé, where he enjoyed the company of the young. On arrival in East Anglia he found a diocese with a scattered Catholic population and with few vocations to the priesthood, and consequently an impending crisis in the number of priests. He reduced the frequency of masses, brought parishes together and closed some unnecessary mass centres. When his plan for the diocese, given the upbeat title *A Community of Welcome*, was published in 2006 it was not greeted warmly by everyone. Michael himself had a mischievous sense of humour and said to those who didn't want change that he would 'throw some chilli peppers into their salad'. That probably didn't help.

I was naïve enough to think that the Catholic laity were naturally obedient to their bishops. This proved to be an Anglican illusion. Soon after his proposals for reorganization were published, Michael telephoned me 'from the bunker', as he described his house and office. The protests didn't all come in green ink, but even Michael was occasionally taken aback by their tone and vehemence. He was accused of being 'a man in a hurry', but he rightly pointed out that he had not caused the hurry and was only facing facts. The structure of the diocese was collapsing. There were just not enough priests. But he did not believe it to be inevitable that there were so few vocations. He committed a good deal of personal energy to fostering vocations. The results may have been relatively modest but by the time of his death there had been an increase in the number of men in training for ordination.

Michael was very aware of the damage that had been done to the confidence of Catholic priests as a result of the sex abuse scandals and all the other crises which seemed to have afflicted the Church in the last generation. Catholic families no longer saw a reason for delight if their children became priests, monks or nuns. Catholic priests themselves rarely commended the priesthood as a fulfilling way of life to young men. The truth was that many of them were lonely themselves, often living an isolated life in a presbytery when they had been trained to live in community with other priests in days when numbers were much greater.

Michael was a bishop who lived in the real world but for whom the joy of being a priest was never lost, whatever the problems to be faced. He found the ministry of a bishop a lonely experience and missed his parish. But the complete integration of Michael's faith, life, work and interests within his priestly ministry was one of the attractive things about him. There was a seamlessness which came from his life in Christ as one of his ministers.

Many people divide their lives between work, leisure, family life, sporting activities, hobbies and all the rest. One of the characteristics of Christian vocation, especially the priesthood, is that the boundaries between these things are entirely porous. The glory of responding to a vocation to the priesthood is to discover that what you do, who you are and what you believe are all so integrated that you cannot separate them. That is why it is a call to give your life away. It was Pope Paul VI, for whom Michael Evans had such devotion, who said 'the priest is a host meant to be broken for his people'. It linked the priest with the broken bread of the Eucharist and Christ's self-offering on the Cross. It was a reminder too that the priest is called to reflect the hospitality of God in Jesus Christ. Michael was the sort of priest and bishop who was at every level a host broken for his people, most of all in his death.

Lord Jesus Christ, our great high priest,
broken on the Cross and raised to new life;
may what we believe, say and do be brought
into unity through you, our blessed Saviour,
the host who invites us to share the heavenly
banquet prepared for all your people. Amen.

39

A Suffering God?

Geoffrey Studdert Kennedy

Mark 15.25–39

When I was ordained in 1975 I recall a discussion at an early deanery chapter about the decline of Remembrance Sunday. It was agreed by every priest present, of whatever age and experience, that its demise was guaranteed once the final veterans of the First World War died out. Those who served in the Second World War seemed to have less connection with it. The servicemen and women of the 1970s were more secular and had little experience of theatres of conflict, except in Northern Ireland. That discussion was an object lesson in the limited predictive powers of the clergy where the future of religion is concerned. No one imagined that 40 years later Remembrance Sunday would generate some of the largest congregations in the Church's year.

The Falklands War marked an initial renewal. The

Gulf War in the early 1990s and a series of later conflicts means that in the last generation there have been few years when the United Kingdom has not been suffering casualties as a result of active service. That is enough to explain the revival of Remembrance Sunday (and of the renewed keeping of the two-minute silence on Armistice Day). No secular replacement for this religious observance has ever been seriously canvassed.

In my early years as a priest, my unseen companion on Remembrance Sunday was Geoffrey Studdert Kennedy. Without his poetry I'm not sure I would have known what to say at that time. His poems were the first to cause me to shed tears as I read them.

In my theological training I had written a passionate defence of the impassibility of God, proving to my satisfaction (and with considerable help from Thomas Aquinas) that God did not suffer. If he did, he would not be God, but a creature subject to the vicissitudes of life like the rest of us. As an exercise in the philosophy of religion it felt like a satisfying intellectual defence. God was unchanging, trans-cendent, immortal, invisible. He was God only wise.

It was what Geoffrey Studdert Kennedy was taught.

It is orthodox Christian belief. The experience of chaplaincy in the First World War, and his encounter with daily death and the serial suffering of the trenches, transformed his whole theological outlook. He became the First World War's most famous padre. He was known to everyone as 'Woodbine Willie' because of his ready distribution of cigarettes:

> They gave me this name like their nature,
> compacted of laughter and tears,
> a sweet that was born of the bitter,
> a joke that was torn from the years.

But it wasn't a name in which he gloried. He felt his response to the men he served was often too superficial:

> Their name! Let me hear it – the symbol
> of unpaid – unpayable debt,
> for the men to whom I owed God's Peace
> I put off with a cigarette.

Studdert Kennedy described his harrowing work crawling from one corpse to another in the trenches reading the burial service and offering a shred of dignity and honour to those whose lives ended in horror, dirt and waste:

And that night I'd been in trenches
seeking out the sodden dead
and just dropping them in shell-holes
with a service swiftly said.

For the bullets rattled round me,
but I couldn't leave them there,
water soaked in flooded shell holes,
reft of common Christian prayer.

A figure emerges with a request of the padre:

Then there spoke a dripping sergeant
when the time was growing late,
'Would you please bury this one,
'Cause 'e used to be my mate?

His mate is a mess of earth and blood, barely recog-
nizable. The service is said. A nearby explosion
lights the face of the grieving sergeant as he stares
at the 'crimson clot of blood', all that's left of his
friend:

There are many kinds of sorrow
in this world of Love and Hate.
But there is no sterner sorrow
than a soldier's for his mate.

Studdert Kennedy returned after the war to the deprived parish of St Paul's, Worcester, to which he had been appointed just as war broke out. In 1922 he moved to London to run St Edmund, Lombard Street, but not to enjoy city life. He was also the public face of the Industrial Christian Fellowship, touring the country, addressing working people, promoting Christian socialism and speaking about the waste of war. The depression of the 1920s seemed poor reward for those who had survived the deprivations of the previous decade. Although a Catholic sacramentalist, Studdert Kennedy had evangelical fervour and sought to take Christ out of confining church buildings. He said, 'nobody worries about Christ as long as he can be kept shut up in churches. He is quite safe there. But there is always trouble if you try to let him out'.

He was giving Lenten addresses in a Liverpool parish when he died in 1929, aged just 45. He was broken in health and disturbed by the triviality of post-war life and the hopeless inadequacy of the Church to meet the needs of the time. The world to which he returned after the war grieved him most. He knew that the suffering Christ identified with suffering humanity, but the gospel was unheard or ignored. Ineffective mission was part of the problem, but human beings had a terrible capacity to neglect what they most needed. His poem 'Indifference' captures the way Christ suffers again:

> When Jesus came to Golgotha they hanged
>   Him on a tree,
> they drave great nails through hands and
>   feet, and made a Calvary;
> they crowned Him with a crown of thorns,
>   red were His wounds and deep,
> for these were crude and cruel days, and
>   human flesh was cheap.
>
> When Jesus came to Birmingham they
>   simply passed Him by,
> they never hurt a hair of Him, they only let
>   Him die;
> for men had grown more tender, and they
>   would not give Him pain,
> they only just passed down the street, and
>   left Him in the rain.
>
> Still Jesus cried, 'Forgive them, for they not
>   what they do',
> and still it rained the wintry rain which
>   drenched Him through and through;
> the crowds went home and left the street
>   without a soul to see,

and Jesus crouched against a wall and cried
    for Calvary.

Lord Jesus, you know the depths of despair and
were nailed to the Cross by human cruelty;
may all who are wounded and heartbroken
know your presence with them and may we all
be brought to your kingdom of peace. Amen.

40

Grief and Love

Victoria James

John 19.25–30

For several years in the 1980s I commuted from our home in Welwyn Garden City to Church House, Westminster. One Friday afternoon in February 1984, walking home from the railway station, I noticed a friend sitting in his car a little way ahead of me. 'That's nice', I thought, 'it will save a ten minute walk'. As I got into the car I could see my friend's face looked very sombre. He told me that our second daughter, Victoria, had died.

She was just over six months old and a victim of Sudden Infant Death Syndrome. There was no explanation, though this was the time when mothers were often told to place children on their tummies when they went to sleep. When that advice changed to placing children on their backs (once avoided because of the fear that a child might choke) the rate of cot deaths went down considerably.

Although all this had happened only two or three hours earlier, by the time I arrived home the police had visited, the doctor had certified death, and Victoria's body had been taken to the mortuary. There was no thought among the professionals for the father who had kissed his daughter goodbye that morning before leaving for work.

Julie and I have often been asked whether we doubted our faith as a result of Victoria's sudden death. There were many difficulties, but, perhaps unusually, that was not one of them. Our strength of faith does not seem related to the happiness of our circumstances. This gave us an experience of grief we would have rather been without. Yet it sensitized us as nothing else seems to do to the sufferings of others. For a long time I could not read newspaper reports of cruelty to children without tears in my eyes.

We often wondered how people came through these things if they were not members of a supportive church community. I had been working at Church House for just a year. We had moved from one side of Welwyn Garden City to the other after I left my former parish. I assisted at St Francis' Church in the centre of the town. It had a vibrant congregation with a wonderful musical tradition, a fine traditional

Catholic priest, Fr Thomas Lloyd Jones, and many young families. We went as usual to the parish mass that Sunday. You could tell that people were surprised to see us there. But Victoria was a child of the Eucharist. There hadn't been a Sunday in her brief life when she had not been part of the Eucharistic community. It is the bread which is broken, Christ's broken body, which is placed into our hands. His broken body is the means of grace so that we may live new lives in him. Brokenness is essential to Eucharistic living. We were broken that day. But at the Eucharist we began to be put back together again.

At Victoria's funeral, a requiem mass for this child of the Eucharist, there were many tears but it struck me even then how many lives she had touched in her brief time on this earth and in the manner of her leaving it. In time it led us to form (with some other local people) a group for parents who had experienced the early deaths of their children. Julie has been a befriender for the Foundation for the Study of Infant Deaths (now the Lullaby Trust) ever since. I have twice preached at a carol service for parents and relatives of children who have died, which takes place each year at York Minster. Hundreds of people attend, many of whom dread the approach of Christmas and the way it reminds them of a child they have lost.

It took years to be able to speak and preach on those and similar occasions. I'd been in Norwich ten years before our daily regional newspaper discovered what happened to us all those years ago, and did an extensive interview on the subject. Perhaps a degree of reserve made the impact more powerful.

Whenever we are asked how many children we have, Julie and I feel guilty not to include Victoria. But when we do and mention that she died you can often see the other person doesn't quite know how to respond. Yet I want to acknowledge her existence and her contribution to my life. Victoria, in her life and death, has shaped and influenced me far more than some of the more famous people I mention in this book.

I never liked it when people referred to Victoria's life 'being cut short'. I know what they meant, but I believe Victoria's life was complete. It was too short for our liking, of course, but her impact on the life of others was greater than some who live a much longer time.

'You can have another child to replace her' – that was the most unthinking comment of all and the one which hurt me most. We did have another child, Dominic. He never replaced Victoria but complemented her in our family where she continues to be remembered and cherished. A child cannot be replaced like a battery or a washing machine as if life is just one more commodity.

The birth of a child brings hope. It isn't simply the promise of a new generation. You see hope in the faces of children. They burn with expectation. Perhaps that's why adults often fall silent in the presence of the new born. It's also why, when a child dies, parents feel that part of them dies too.

Adults are sometimes surprised by the power of a new-born baby. When our first child, Rebecca, was born, she changed our world. Our social life was reconfigured. Everything we did was planned to fit around the smallest member of the family. This tiny baby had huge power over us. The authority of a child is intriguing to ponder. God chooses this way to reveal himself to us.

It seems absurd that God should become a weak and defenceless infant, living a human life. This child called Jesus still fascinates, and speaks of the wonder of love to billions. He grew into a man, and while Joseph disappears from the story, his mother stays with him. She sees her son die agonizingly – and innocent – on the Cross. Mary knew what it was to be a bereaved parent. Holy Saturday was for her a day of desolation. If, as Christians have always believed, her son was the Son of God, then God himself knows the experience of a bereaved parent too. And that is the greatest mystery of all.

> *God of the heartbroken, look with compassion*
> *on all bereaved parents, and sustain them*
> *in the knowledge that you have shared their*
> *experience in the death of your Son Jesus*
> *Christ. Amen.*

CONCLUSION

Matthew, Mark and Luke all consider the names of the 12 disciples of Jesus sufficiently important to list them in their gospels. Their name is the one and only piece of reliable information we have about some disciples – Bartholomew, for example. The Twelve were not disciples in general. Each had a particular identity. Named witnesses to the Resurrection were equally important. Luke records that the risen Christ appeared on the Emmaus road to a disciple called Cleopas (not one of the Twelve). He is sometimes identified with Clopas, whose wife Mary goes with the other women to the tomb in John's gospel, but we cannot be sure. Later in the story, but still before the coming of the Holy Spirit, it is decided to replace Judas as one of the Twelve with another apostle. There were two named candidates: Joseph called Barsabbas (also known as Justus), and the rather more straightforwardly named Matthias. Matthias is chosen by lot. Whether he had a fruitful ministry or not we do not know. We never hear of him again.

A religion grounded in the incarnation, the enfleshment of God in human form, gives individual human identity significance. Names are highly personal. You cannot be baptized without a name. Names carry our identity. Jesus was rather keen on renaming his disciples or giving them nicknames. Simon became Peter, the rock. James and John, explosive characters as they were, were called *Boarneges* meaning *Sons of Thunder*. Instead of getting this volatile pair to undertake a Myers-Briggs personality profile, Jesus simply gives them a suitable nickname. Perhaps they had the self-awareness to reflect on Jesus' joke. Even Simon's new name seems ironic when you think of his threefold denial that he even knew Jesus. Perhaps only someone so well acquainted with the fallen character of his humanity could have been the rock on whom the Church would be built.

Christians in every generation have remembered their companions in faith by name. Our churches and churchyards are littered with memorials. As time goes on, only the recorded name remains. The living community, worshipping in ancient church buildings, is often surrounded by the names of those already long dead before any of the present congregation was born. It does not render the departed insignificant. Some of those in this book have such memorials. Others are unrecorded anywhere but are no less significant to God.

The companions Jesus chose at the beginning of his ministry seem to have been picked almost at random. They were given no job description about what being a disciple would mean. They were put through no discernment process. Jesus simply said 'come, follow me'. The imperative of God was enough in itself. There must have been something compelling about Jesus for James and John to leave their livelihood as fishermen and go off with him. (The gospels do not record what Zebedee, their father, made of Jesus taking away his workforce.) The consequences of becoming a companion of Jesus led Peter to Rome. According to tradition, Thomas went to India whereas Andrew ends up, rather surprisingly, as the patron saint of Scotland. The very localized ministry Jesus exercised in Galilee, followed by a brief time in Jerusalem, turns out to be of world significance. Ordinary inhabitants of Galilee were led by faith in Christ to do extraordinary things. Becoming a companion of Jesus Christ can mean costly adventures for believers in every age. Edith Cavell, Joseph Hall or Geoffrey Studdert Kennedy would be examples from this book. Some stories here also illustrate why we know the names of some of the first Christians and nothing more about them. Many early disciples did not go on to be martyrs or world travellers. Not all were in the front line of persecution. Their witness to

Jesus Christ may have been wholly contained within the routines of domestic and local community life. That's been true for most Christians down the ages. Phyllis Simmons, Edith James and Michael Stagg among others remind us of the way we see God at work in those who live around us and minister to us. Such people are the rocks on whom the Church of Jesus Christ has been built.

Around 20 of my companions chose themselves very easily. Over several months others came into my mind one by one, sometimes almost spontaneously. It struck me how much I owed to the writings of a poet (U. A. Fanthorpe), the support and Christian courtesy of a friend (Robin Ferrers) or the lasting impact of a place and a person (Bernard Walke). It also dawned on me that no fewer than 12 of these companions would not have been included prior to my becoming Bishop of Norwich in 1999. I have now lived in Norwich longer than any other place during my life. I have become a tiny part of its history myself. While some of my Norwich companions come from centuries past (George Borrow and Edward Reynolds), four of them have died in the past decade. Our formation as Christian disciples continues into the later decades of our lives. The journey of faith with fellow pilgrims on the way is one of continuing new discoveries.

The word *companion* means one with whom you share bread. Many of the companions in this book shared regularly, during their lives, in the breaking of bread around the Lord's Table. The vast majority of Christians also share meals in their homes and elsewhere with people of different faith traditions or none. Eating together is a form of communion in itself, deepening friendships and understanding, and broadening our sympathies. It's a common-place way in almost every culture of getting to know the stranger and offering a welcome.

Christians may have a particular understanding of what it is to be a companion of Jesus Christ but that does not blind them to seeing the grace and mercy of God at work in those who do not share their faith. That's why this book has included people such as Hugo Gryn, John Lyttle or Kathleen Ferrier who would not have been found around the Table of the Lord, though Hugo certainly understood the significance of that meal for Christians. God's grace isn't confined by the sacraments. Instead, the sacraments help us to see that grace is more widespread than we can conceive. Our eyes are opened to the sacramental character of a world in which God is present in a rich and diverse creation and in the human beings he has made. The sacramental Christian rejoices in an abundance of grace, and keeps being surprised by God's revelation of himself in unlikely places and unlikely people.

The Australian poet Judith Wright captures the intoxication of the discovery of God's grace in human life in one of her poems, simply called 'Grace':

> Living is dailiness, a simple bread
> That's worth the eating. But I have known
>   a wine,
> a drunkenness that can't be spoken or sung
> without betraying it. Far past Yours or
>   Mine,
> even past Ours, it has nothing at all to say;
> it slants a sudden laser through common
>   day.
>
> It seems to have nothing to do with things
>   at all,
> requires another element or dimension.
> Not contemplation brings it; it merely
>   happens,
> past expectation and beyond intention;
> takes over the depth of flesh, the inward eye,
> is there, then vanishes. Does not live or die.
>
> Because it occurs beyond the here and now,
> positives, negatives, what we hope and are.

Not even being in love, or making love,
brings it. It plunges a sword from a dark
　　star.

Maybe there was once a word for it. Call it
　　grace.
I have seen it, once or twice, through a
　　human face.

ACKNOWLEDGMENTS

This book would not have been written without encouragement from Caroline Chartres at Bloomsbury, whose expertise, good humour and wise advice along the way has been invaluable. I am grateful also to Jamie Birkett, her colleague and Kim Storry and other staff at Fakenham Prepress Solutions.

My PA, Coralie Nichols, has been an immense support in ensuring the book took shape and played an important part in proofreading and correcting errors. Any that remain are my own responsibility.

There are many others who are unaware that they have made any contribution to this book but whose stray remarks about a poet, artist, priest or friend have lodged in my mind and found a home in one or other of the chapters here. To them I owe a debt for enlarging my understanding of what it means to be a Christian disciple.